A DK PUBLISHING BOOK
www.dk.com

Art Editor Goldberry Broad

Editors David Pickering, Nick Turpin, Caryn Jenner

Managing Art Editor Cathy Tincknell

Managing Editor Joanna Devereux

US Editor Constance Robinson

Photographers Andy Crawford, Erik Andreson

DTP Designers Kim Browne, Jill Bunyan

Production Steve Lang

Picture Research Anna Grapes, Andy Sansom

First American Edition, 1999

2 4 6 8 10 9 7 5 3 1

Published in the United States by
DK Publishing Inc.
95 Madison Avenue
New York, New York 10016

A catalog record for this book is available from the Library of Congress

ISBN 0-7894-4691-X

Color reproduction by Colourscan, Singapore
Printed and bound in Slovakia by Neografia

The
Ultimate
LEGO
Book

A DK PUBLISHING BOOK

www.dk.com

CONTENTS

THE LEGO STORY

LEGO MASTER BUILDERS

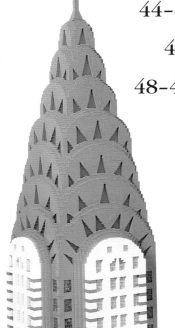

LEGOLANDS – THE PARKS

IMAGINATION UNLIMITED

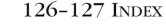

FOREWORD

This book is not about a toy. It is a book about an idea, a set of values, and a long-term commitment to empowering children to use their creativity and build their imagination.

When my grandfather, Ole Kirk Christiansen, started producing wooden toys in 1932, his maxim was "only the best is good enough." Way back when my grandfather coined this phrase, it was basically a statement of quality referring to good workmanship. So, the LEGO toys were carefully crafted and given three coats of paint – quite unusual in those days.

Today, however, "quality" has a much broader dimension, and what really sets companies apart is the value and thinking behind the actual product. LEGO products are still produced with the greatest attention to detail, based on research into children's development stages and play patterns.

All LEGO branded products are conceived to stimulate children in various ways. On their own, the products are only the raw material – they cannot come to life without the vital spark of a child's creativity and imagination.

Whether it is a LEGO set, a LEGOLAND park or a LEGO software game, the experience is never passive entertainment – the child is the main actor and learns while playing.

Children are our vital concern. Our aim is to stimulate children to become masters of their own lives – not by giving them finished solutions, but by giving them tools to manipulate and challenges to solve, and by enticing their natural curiosity … the same way they are learning through life.

We plan to become the strongest brand for families with children by the year 2005. Not the biggest, but the best. To achieve this ambition, a range of exciting new initiatives are being taken in the LEGO Group to introduce LEGO values into new areas of children's lives, all of which you can read more about in *The Ultimate LEGO Book* … and I am sure that by looking behind the scenes of our company, you will realize that working here not only takes the best practical skills – it also involves a lot of exuberance and imagination.

My father, Godtfred, made a giant leap for the company when he patented the LEGO brick in 1958. By creating the LEGO System, he created the platform for the LEGO play materials we know today. Over the years we have extended and developed this platform further, and today children play with the programmable LEGO brick, creating wonderful wacky LEGO robots and sharing their ideas and models with children on the other side of the globe via the Internet.

You may wonder: where will this lead to?

How will this new kind of play help children understand technology and prepare them for their future?

Just imagine …

Kjeld Kirk Kristiansen, President & CEO, LEGO Group

A World All Its Own

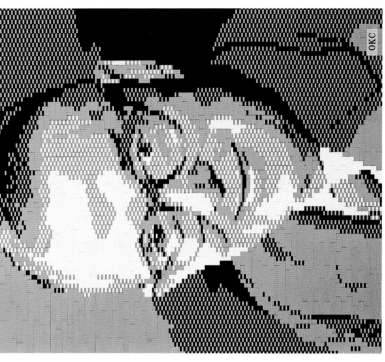

OKC

THE LEGO COMPANY began by making many wooden toys. It now produces a wide range of products for children to which the LEGO brick is central, and all of which fit into the same system of play. It has been estimated that by 1996 about 180 *billion* LEGO elements had been produced, and that 300 million children and adults all over the world either play or have played with LEGO bricks. Every year, children spend almost 5 billion hours playing with LEGO bricks – that is almost one hour for every human being on Earth! With a few bricks and a little imagination a child can create almost anything; this book documents just some of the highways of creativity that the world of LEGO bricks has revealed.

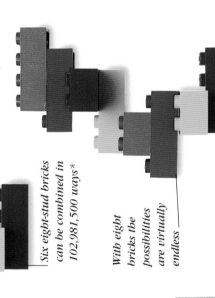

BUILT TO LAST

The sky is no limit! Professional LEGO model makers have built this 21-ft 6-in (620-cm) tall version of the Empire State Building and dozens of other world-famous landmarks using the same bricks and techniques available to the youngest LEGO modeler. Of course, most modelers can only dream of having this many LEGO bricks to play with.

Two eight-stud LEGO bricks can be combined in 24 ways*

Three eight-stud bricks can be combined in 1,060 ways*

Six eight-stud bricks can be combined in 102,981,500 ways*

With eight bricks the possibilities are virtually endless

THE KEY TO IT ALL

The unique way that LEGO bricks combine is the basis for every LEGO product. Bricks can be fitted together in an extraordinary number of ways. Using different color bricks multiplies the numbers of possible combinations even further.

* This only works if all bricks are the same color

This model took 782 hours to build and contains about 175,000 bricks

Ole Kirk Christiansen
(1891–1958)

The Story of a Family

The LEGO company has always been owned and run by the Kirk Christiansen family. Ole Kirk Christiansen began to make toys in 1932 and ran his own company until his death in 1958. His son, Godtfred Kirk Christiansen, then took over. On his becoming Chairman in 1979, his eldest son, Kjeld Kirk Kristiansen, became President and still runs the LEGO Group today.

Godtfred Kirk Christiansen (1920–1995)

Kjeld Kirk Kristiansen (b.1947) His name is spelled with a K because the priest made a mistake when entering it in the church annals

This robot is programmed to throw balls down holes

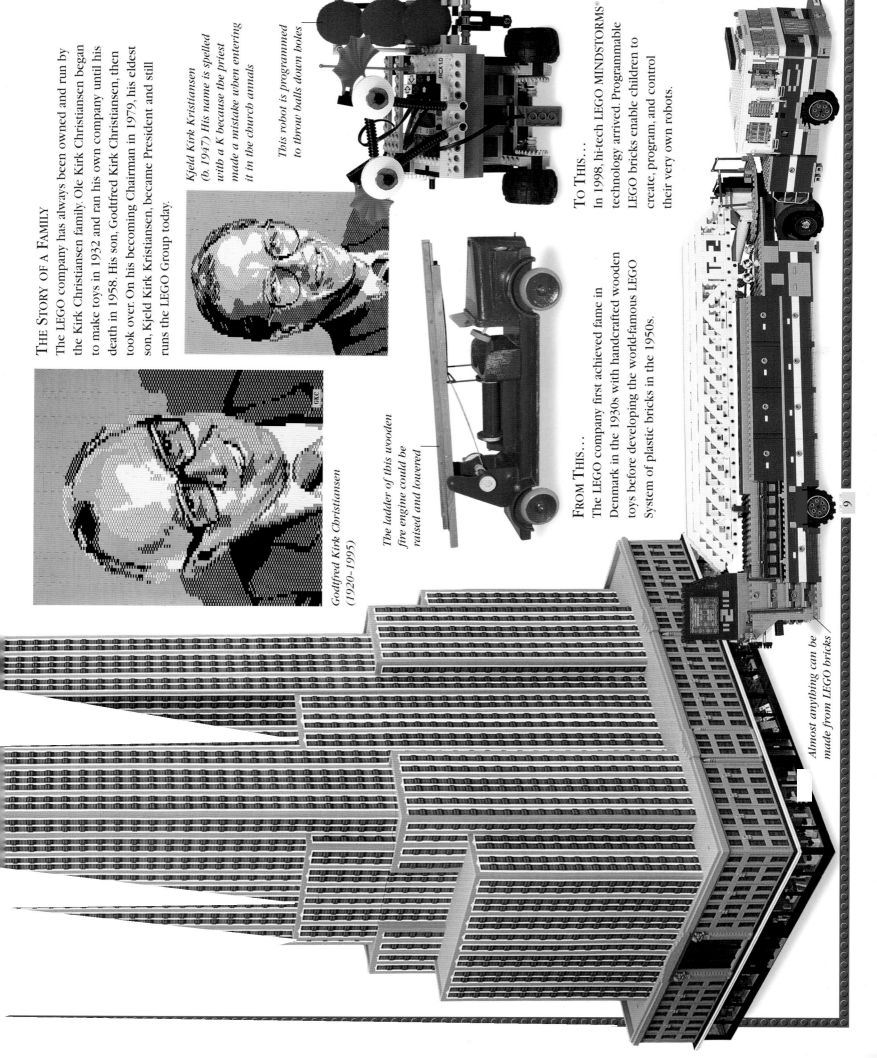

To This…
In 1998, hi-tech LEGO MINDSTORMS® technology arrived. Programmable LEGO bricks enable children to create, program, and control their very own robots.

The ladder of this wooden fire engine could be raised and lowered

From This…
The LEGO company first achieved fame in Denmark in the 1930s with handcrafted wooden toys before developing the world-famous LEGO System of plastic bricks in the 1950s.

Almost anything can be made from LEGO bricks

WORK HARD, PLAY WELL

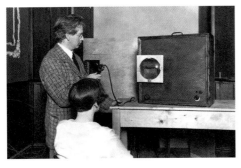

THE STORY OF THE LEGO GROUP begins with a remarkable man. Ole Kirk Christiansen was a master carpenter and joiner in the small town of Billund, in Jutland, Denmark. In 1932, the Great Depression was affecting his business badly, and he decided to diversify into making household products and wooden toys. Had there been no economic depression, he might just have stayed a carpenter and the plastic LEGO brick might never have been created.

CHANGING TIMES
Ole Kirk was born in 1891, just six years after Karl Benz made the first car. He died in 1958, one year after the first satellite went into space.

TECHNOLOGICAL STRIDES
In 1926, the first black-and-white television was invented. Six years later the first wooden LEGO toys were made.

This sign was carved by Ole Kirk himself

A LASTING MOTTO
Ole Kirk's motto was "Only the best is good enough" (left, in Danish). He never skimped on quality or allowed his employees to do so.

HUMBLE HAMLET
When Ole Kirk first lived in Billund, there were only eight houses. His family had deep roots in the area and they and their company have never moved away.

In 1942, when all production patterns were lost in a fire, Ole Kirk remade them by hand

"LIFE IS A GIFT, BUT ALSO A TASK"
The Christiansen family were members of a Danish Christian movement called Indre Mission. Ole Kirk's faith gave him a sense of duty; as he saw it, life was a gift but also a task. His faith helped him through personal crises, including the death of his wife in 1932, which left him with four young sons to look after.

LEGO
BILLUND ★ DENMARK

THE STORY BEHIND THE NAME

In 1934, Ole Kirk held a competition among his staff to find a name for his company. The prize was a bottle of wine. He won it himself with "LEGO," which is a contraction of the Danish for "play well" – "LEg GOdt."

SOLO PIONEER

In 1932, the same year that Ole Kirk began to make toys, Amelia Earhart became the first woman to fly solo across the Atlantic. The world was changing fast.

This 1930s portrait shows company employees displaying their work.

A GROWING REPUTATION

LEGO toys acquired a reputation for quality and durability in Denmark. These wooden cars were designed by Godtfred Kirk Christiansen in the late 1930s.

PRECISION TOOLS

The company's commitment to quality led to investment in the latest machinery. This milling machine (left) was bought in Germany in the mid-1930s.

The LEGO sign over the factory door; incidentally, "lego" is the Latin word for "I assemble," or "I put together"

FROM THE ASHES

In 1942, a fire destroyed the factory, and Ole Kirk's life work. In the ensuing months, he drove himself to rebuild it all.

From the outset, the LEGO company's toys were full of charm and personality

TEDDY BIL

HIGH STANDARDS

Once, Ole Kirk's son Godtfred decided to save company money by giving the toy ducks two coats of paint instead of three. His father told him: "Go and get the ducks immediately, give them their last coat of paint, repack them, and take them back to the station. And do it all yourself – even if it takes you all night!"

This pull-along duck was one of the most popular wooden LEGO toys from the mid-1930s to the late 1940s

LEGO

A SYSTEM OF PLAY

AFTER THE WAR, new plastics technology meant that totally new kinds of toys could be made. The LEGO company began producing plastic products in 1947 and two years later, Godtfred Kirk Christiansen (GKC), Ole Kirk's son, pioneered the first forerunners of LEGO bricks, Automatic Binding Bricks. Then, in 1954, he perceived a huge gap in the toy market: there was no *system* of play available for children – only individual toys. In an inspired moment he realized that the LEGO brick could fill that gap.

One of the first plastic toys was a baby's rattle, designed by GKC

NEW TECHNOLOGY
The LEGO company was the first in Denmark to buy a molding machine for injecting plastics.

DAYS OF HOPE
World War II ended in 1945. Normal life begins again and people start building for the future.

The top of the brick already has the LEGO look

There was no binding mechanism underneath

Early bricks would not keep their shape

ANCESTORS OF THE LEGO BRICK
Automatic Binding Bricks were made in 1949. They did not yet possess the unique binding mechanism that defines true LEGO bricks.

1949 FIRST BRICKS

Colors were similar to those on today's bricks, but they tended to fade

In the postwar period, raw materials for plastics were expensive and hard to obtain

THE PRICE OF SUCCESS
The cost of plastic toys was high but so was Ole Kirk's belief in their possibilities. "If we get this right," he said, "we can sell these toys all over the world." By 1951, plastic toys accounted for half the company's output.

1951's Ferguson tractor was one of the company's first successes with a plastic toy

EARLY DAYS
In the 1950s The LEGO company was still a small business; everyone knew each other, and almost everyone met for a short prayer meeting before work.

NEW NAME

The new binding bricks were renamed "LEGO bricks" in 1953.

Larger vehicles made by the company

The boy in the white shirt is Kjeld Kirk Kristiansen, now the LEGO group's president and its main shareholder

NEW SOUNDS

While the LEGO System develops, rock 'n' roll is born. In 1955, Bill Haley and the Comets' record "Rock Around the Clock" becomes a big hit.

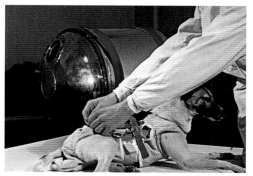

FIRST IN SPACE

In October 1957, the Soviet Union sent Sputnik I, the first satellite, into space. In November a dog named Laika became the first living being to travel there.

1953 FIRST BASE FOR BUILDING

1954 FIRST BEAM BRICK

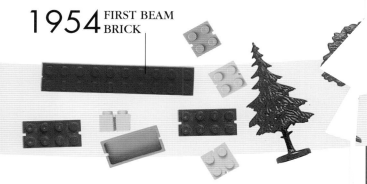

1955 FIRST LEGO TREES

A NEW TOY

In 1955, the company launched the "LEGO System of Play": the Town Plan line. Sets contained buildings, trees, cars, and signs, so that a whole town could be built. The System ensured that all the elements fitted together. The philosophy behind this revolutionary toy was clearly stated: "Our idea has been to create a toy that appeals to children's imagination and develops the urge to create."

The Town Plan's modern setting helped children learn about traffic safety

There were 28 sets and eight vehicles in the line

Kjeld was a big fan of LEGO bricks from the start

A Perfect Fit

THE STUD-AND-TUBE coupling system for LEGO bricks was invented in 1957 and marketed in 1958. It enabled children to build models of considerable complexity with ease. Following a fire in the warehouse of wooden toys, the company decided to concentrate all its resources on realizing the enormous potential of the plastic LEGO brick.

A Historic Document

In 1958, a patent was sought for the final LEGO stud-and-tube coupling system. It has proved one of the most valuable ever granted. Over the years, many companies have tried to imitate LEGO bricks.

The stud-and-tube-coupling system gave extra impetus to LEGO in the 1960s

1957 FIRST LEGO FLAGS

1958 FIRST STUD-AND-TUBE COUPLING BRICK

1957 FIRST LIGHTS

1957 FIRST LEGO WINDOW

1962 FIRST WHEEL

The Future Is Plastic

In February 1960, a fire in the wooden-toy department brought production of wooden toys to a halt. Henceforth the company decided to focus all its resources on making plastic toys. This photograph, taken at that time, is of the plastic moldings factory in Billund.

A joint links the wheel to the other LEGO bricks, a simple yet strong and durable design

The Invention of the Wheel

In 1961, the LEGO Company invented the wheel. The following year, the first LEGO wheels hit the shops. Today the LEGO Group makes more tires than any other company in the world.

The First Spaceman

It is a historic moment when Russian cosmonaut Yuri Gagarin becomes the first human to go into space in 1961, fueling world interest in science and technology.

COMPANY AND COMMUNITY

By 1962, the growth of the company meant that it needed an airfield at Billund. That year an airstrip was built in a field bordered by giant LEGO bricks. With the local government's help, the strip later became a public airport serving a large area of western Denmark. GKC guaranteed the airport for its first few years.

A NEW PRECISION

In 1963, the LEGO company found a better material for its bricks. Cellulose acetate was replaced by ABS (acrylnitrile butadiene styrene). The new material was more stable, more color-fast, and allowed greater molding precision, to 0.0002 inm (0.005 m).

THE FAB FOUR

In 1965 in the UK, the Beatles collect an MBE from the Queen, reflecting the decade's faith in youth and enterprise.

EVER MORE ELEMENTS

By 1966, the LEGO product line comprised 57 sets and 25 vehicles. A total of 706 million elements was produced during the year.

1962 FIRST 1/3 ELEMENT

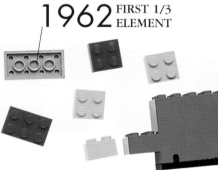

1966 TRAIN MOTOR

ENGINEERING TOOL

1963 saw the launch of MODULEX®, which allowed adults to build scale models of real buildings. Here, GKC examines a model of the Billund air terminal.

ON THE RIGHT TRACK

The first of many journeys by a LEGO train began in 1966. A 4.5-volt motor was launched at the same time, so that children could have power for their trains if they wanted it; in 1969, 12-volt motors were added to the line.

Railroad signs

PARKS AND PEOPLE

I N 1968, THE FIRST LEGOLAND park was established in Billund, and after ten years of a "System of Play," the LEGO company had become a force to be reckoned with. GKC was determined to maintain this impetus and insisted that "The LEGO System must offer unlimited play possibilities." With new product development the focus, a host of exciting new series burst onto the market.

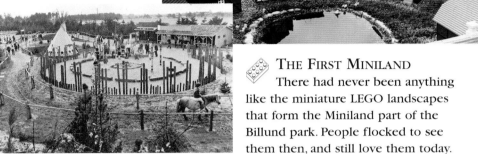

THE FIRST MINILAND
There had never been anything like the miniature LEGO landscapes that form the Miniland part of the Billund park. People flocked to see them then, and still love them today.

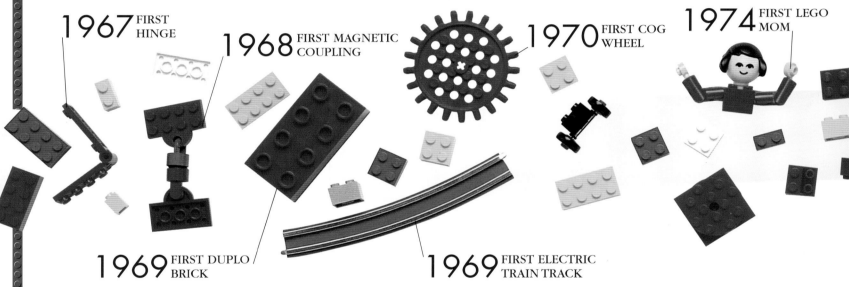

1967 FIRST HINGE

1968 FIRST MAGNETIC COUPLING

1970 FIRST COG WHEEL

1974 FIRST LEGO MOM

1969 FIRST DUPLO BRICK

1969 FIRST ELECTRIC TRAIN TRACK

WALKING ON THE MOON
American astronaut Neil Armstrong becomes the first man on the Moon, on July 20, 1969. With the words, "That's one small step for man, one giant leap for mankind," he steps down from Apollo 11 onto the surface.

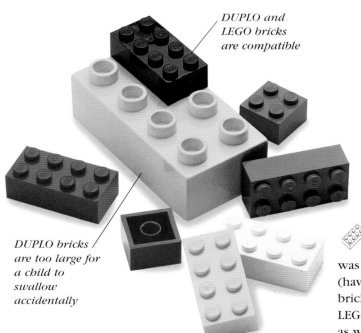

DUPLO and LEGO bricks are compatible

DUPLO bricks are too large for a child to swallow accidentally

078
LEGO
PreSchool

32 interlocking pieces
Store these building blocks in this box

BIG BRICKS FOR TINY FINGERS
The DUPLO® series for under-fives was launched internationally in 1969 (having been invented in 1967). DUPLO bricks are eight times bigger than basic LEGO bricks – twice as long, twice as wide, and twice as high.

A New Logo
In 1973, a single new logo took the place of the various logos that had existed before. All the company's products thus became unified under one banner.

Terra-cotta Army
In 1975, an army of 6,000 life-size terra-cotta warriors is unearthed at Xian, the ancient capital of China. Each warrior has an individual face. They guard the tomb of the emperor Qin Shi Huangdi, who first unified China. He died in 206 BC.

People For Lego World
Having invented an entire world, the LEGO Group naturally would create people to fill it. In 1974 LEGO figures were launched, starting with the LEGO family. The figures were soon the biggest-selling product, loved as much by girls as by boys.

Other elements can be attached to hands

Legs cannot move

1977 DUPLO PEOPLE

1977 TECHNIC PLATE WITH HOLES

1977 TECHNIC GEAR WHEEL

Kjeld's Way
In the late 1970s Kjeld Kirk Kristiansen formulated a concept to introduce "system into the System." This later led to LEGO "themes" such as Pirate, Space, and Castle.

People Power
Adding figures to LEGO sets increased their appeal, especially for younger children.

The First Ship
The first LEGO ship designed to float was launched in 1973.

The Real Thing
The LEGO TECHNIC® series, launched in 1977, allowed older children to make motorized mechanical models.

SERIOUS FUN

I N THE EARLY 1980s, the LEGO Group further extended its lines by focusing on education. A separate Educational Products Division was set up to develop toys especially for use in schools and kindergartens, and by handicapped children. Today, this division is known as LEGO Dacta. These years also saw the successful launch of themes such as LEGO Space and LEGO Castle.

THERE AND BACK
In 1977, the US Space Shuttle, the first reusable spacecraft, completes its initial test flight.

INTO SPACE
Space exploration was headline news in the late 1970s, and the Space set proved to be the LEGO Group's greatest success so far.

1979 FIRST SPACE KIT

1980 RAILROAD TIE

1980 ELECTRIC TRAIN TRACKS

1978 FIRST FLEXIBLE MINI FIGURE

1980 LEGO TECHNIC SHOCK ABSORBER

FLEXIBLE FRIENDS
In 1978, Mini figures with movable limbs and hands that could grasp toy utensils were launched. They became the company's second most important design, after the LEGO brick itself.

By 1998, 2.3 billion of these Mini figures had been made

PERSONAL COMPUTER
By the late 1970s, new microchip technology means that computers can be produced for personal use.

FABULOUS FABULAND
The FABULAND® line was launched in 1979. The pieces were large and easily assembled. The series featured a number of animal characters, whose adventures were told in accompanying booklets.

Ricky Bear - a 1980s character

ROMANCE OF THE ROAD
The Vintage Car series launched in 1975 was not a bestseller. Nostalgia for the great days of driving had little appeal for 1970s children.

Studs connect to other DUPLO pieces so that really inventive rattles can be made

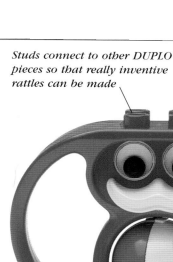

FEED THE WORLD!
In 1985, pop stars in Britain and the US perform at the massive Live Aid concerts organized by Bob Geldof to raise money for the victims of a terrible famine in Ethiopia.

FOR CHILDREN
I April 1985, the LEGO Prize was founded, which is an international annual award for exceptional efforts on behalf of children anywhere in the world.

BABY TOYS
The DUPLO Baby series, including six double-grip rattles, came out in 1983.

1982 BATTERY BOX

1984 CASTLE KNIGHTS' PENNANT

1982 WIND-UP ENGINE

This 1978 forerunner of the LEGO Castle series was yellow; later castles were more realistic in gray and black

1985 GEARSTICK

MAGIC REALMS
The LEGO Castle series, introduced in 1984, showed that LEGO toys could colonize magical worlds of sword and sorcery, too.

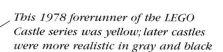

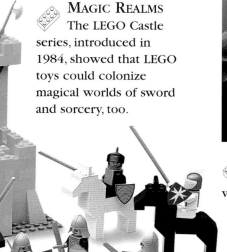

COMPUTER CONTROL
LEGO TECHNIC robots controlled via computer were launched in schools in 1986. In the same year, electronic Light and Sound sets were launched for the LEGO Town and LEGO Space kits.

FULL SPEED AHEAD

PIRATES LED THE WAY for the LEGO Group at the end of the 1980s; the LEGO pirates product line became the most successful so far. Ideas continued to flow, with kits such as a DUPLO zoo and new lines of TECHNIC cars. There was also a move into licensed products, starting with children's clothes. The first official LEGO World Cup building championship took place in 1988, underscoring the company's international status. The headquarters remained at Billund, despite the fact that most of the products were sold outside Denmark.

Yo Ho Ho!
Eleven LEGO Pirates sets were launched in 1989, with ships and forts; it became the most successful product line yet.

1987 CONDUCTOR BRICK

1988 BRICK SEPARATOR

1989 PIRATES' PARROT

1990 PULL-BACK MOTOR

1986 LEGO LIGHTS

THE WALL FALLS
For many years after the end of World War II, Europe was divided by the conflict known as the Cold War between the former Soviet Union and the West. In 1989, peaceful revolutions in eastern Europe end the conflict. The Berlin Wall, which divided that city, is torn down.

MODEL TEAM
A line of ever more realistic sets came out through the late 1980s and early 1990s. This Model Team set of 1990 enabled children to build a truck, a trailer, and a helicopter.

DUPLO ZOO
One of of the most successful launches of 1990 was the DUPLO Zoo. Fifteen species of animals were produced.

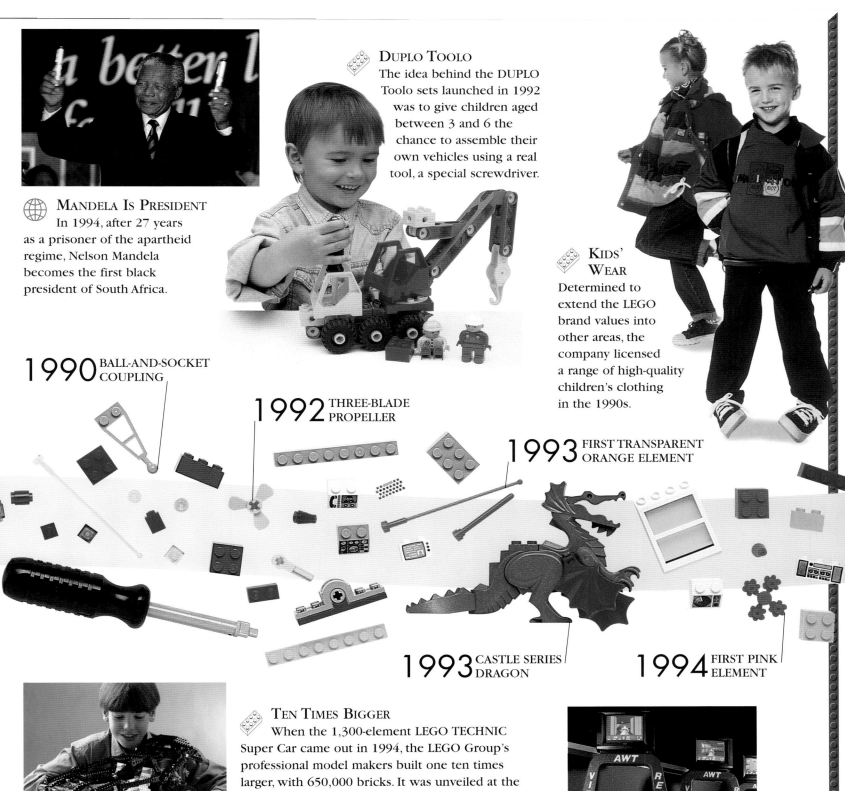

DUPLO TOOLO
The idea behind the DUPLO Toolo sets launched in 1992 was to give children aged between 3 and 6 the chance to assemble their own vehicles using a real tool, a special screwdriver.

MANDELA IS PRESIDENT
In 1994, after 27 years as a prisoner of the apartheid regime, Nelson Mandela becomes the first black president of South Africa.

KIDS' WEAR
Determined to extend the LEGO brand values into other areas, the company licensed a range of high-quality children's clothing in the 1990s.

1990 BALL-AND-SOCKET COUPLING

1992 THREE-BLADE PROPELLER

1993 FIRST TRANSPARENT ORANGE ELEMENT

1993 CASTLE SERIES DRAGON

1994 FIRST PINK ELEMENT

TEN TIMES BIGGER
When the 1,300-element LEGO TECHNIC Super Car came out in 1994, the LEGO Group's professional model makers built one ten times larger, with 650,000 bricks. It was unveiled at the "Mondial de l'Automobile 1994" exhibition in Paris.

SEEING THE FUTURE?
The early 1990s see the development of 3-D simulations so convincing they are called "virtual reality." Suddenly children can go out to play in another dimension!

A World Leader

A NEW PARK every three years around the world: this is the LEGO Group's vision for LEGOLAND® parks. The concept began in 1968 in Billund, followed by LEGOLAND Windsor in England in 1996, and LEGOLAND California in 1999. Meanwhile, the LEGO SYSTEM and LEGO TECHNIC series continued to develop: in 1997 there were 542 different sets, and 1,964 different molded elements. LEGO books and CD-ROMs joined the products series. Led by Kjeld Kirk Kristiansen's vision of how to develop the play materials' market, and supported by a wish to develop new areas for the Group, LEGO became one of the world's leading brands for children.

LEGO PRIMO
A new series called LEGO PRIMO®, especially designed for the under-twos, was launched in 1995.

Clarence Caterpillar

1995 FIRST DOLPHIN

PLAYING FOR TIME
Joining the ever-growing range of licensed products in 1996 was the unique LEGO WATCH SYSTEM®.

1996 RACING CAR NUMBER

BEST WESTERN
The Western kit, launched in 1996, brought the wild west to LEGO fans. The series featured characters such as Colonel Jefferson of Fort Apache.

ROYAL NEIGHBORS
The Windsor LEGOLAND park opened in the UK in 1996, within sight of HM the Queen's Windsor Castle. It had over a million visitors in its first year.

NO LIMITS

The ever-expanding LEGO SYSTEM line saw the Adventurers and Insectoids product lines launched in 1998, and Rock Raiders in 1999.

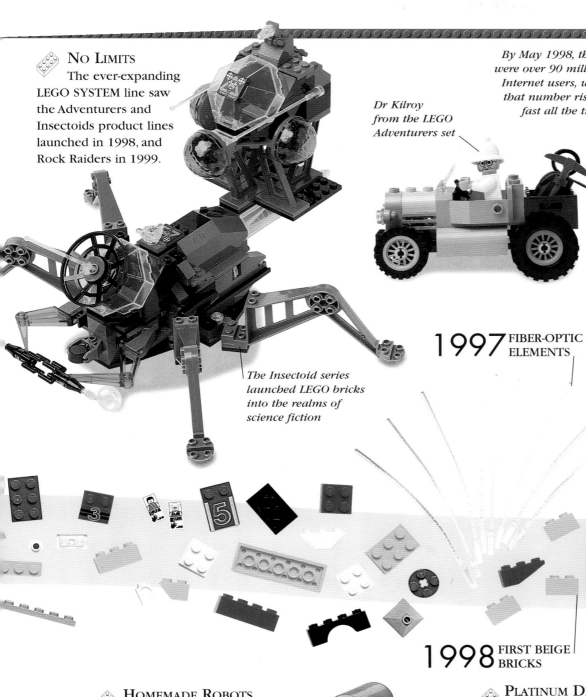

The Insectoid series launched LEGO bricks into the realms of science fiction

Dr Kilroy from the LEGO Adventurers set

By May 1998, there were over 90 million Internet users, with that number rising fast all the time

WORLD ON-LINE

Perhaps the most important technological development of the 1990s is the Internet, which enables people to write, chat, and research information – in fact, communicate in almost any way. The LEGO Company now has its own Website.

1997 FIBER-OPTIC ELEMENTS

1999 ROCK RAIDERS MONSTER

1998 FIRST BEIGE BRICKS

1998 CREATOR CD-ROM

HOMEMADE ROBOTS

Developed with scientists and educators at Massachusetts Institute of Technology and launched in 1998 in the US and Britain, LEGO MINDSTORMS® enabled children to build and program robots using a computer.

The robot's arm can move items, such as this soft-drink can

PLATINUM DISC

The first computer game, LEGO Island, was launched in 1997, and became a worldwide hit, selling nearly a million copies in its first year. Its success was followed by other games, such as LEGO Creator, LEGO Loco, and LEGO Chess, in 1998.

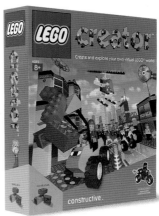

COMING TO AMERICA

After years of planning, LEGOLAND California opened in Carlsbad in 1999. The picture (left) shows San Francisco in the park's Miniland.

A LEGO LIFESTYLE

T HE LEGO GROUP'S determination to become a leading family brand means that it has extended its lines beyond the LEGO brick. By licensing a wide series of clothing and accessories, the company has created an entire lifestyle for today's children. Of course, any product bearing the LEGO name must also represent the company's values of play and safety, and be of the highest quality.

BAGS OF FUN
The LEGO Container System consists of 15 types of bag, covering every kind a child might need from school bags, backpacks, and sports bags to pencil cases and wallets.

Removable bag can be used as a belt bag

Strap adjusts to fit even the smallest wrist

Strap elements clip together easily and are quickly changed

Thick mineral glass

Water-resistant to 100 ft (30 meters)

All bags are strong, durable, and washable

BRILLIANT BOOTS!
The LEGO rubber boot line is called Mudhoppers. Designed for fun and comfort, they are manufactured with cushioned, washable insoles, cotton linings, and high-quality natural rubber.

Cushioned insole for extra comfort

Colors are based on the look of the UFO series

Slippers are light and flexible with antislip soles – vital for safe play

Outer rings have various timing functions

There are plenty of spare links

TIME TO CHANGE
The LEGO WATCH SYSTEM is a high-quality, build-it-yourself watch whose parts can be easily changed to create a completely different look every day.

FASHIONABLE AND FUNCTIONAL
LEGO Kids Wear is designed to be fun, functional, and comfortable. It is specially developed for play: the practical fastenings make clothes easy to put on and take off; there are no itchy materials, uncomfortable seams, or tight elastic. Colors are fully tested for fastness and all outer wear is developed to keep the cold out and the warmth in.

Detachable hood

Soft natural fabrics retain shape

This skisuit's numerous features include Velcro fastening at the neck, a breast pocket with zipper, and reflecting labels

Adjustable sleeves

Sturdy pockets with press-button fastening

Reinforcing patch

Reflecting band

Clothing designed to allow freedom of movement and durability

LEGO Kids Wear caters for all age groups from babies to ten-year-olds

Combed cotton yarns prevent pilling

Strong cotton yarns used for longer-lasting look and comfort

Soft denim material selected for maximum comfort

MEDIA MAGIC

IMAGINE NEW WAYS to play! LEGO MEDIA has. The LEGO MEDIA division develops exciting computer software using the key elements of LEGO toys in a new way. Among other things, each CD-ROM is carefully tested with both children and adults to ensure endless potential for creativity and fun. With LEGO CD-ROMs, you can build things (and knock them down, too), play games, and learn new skills.

Symbol for LEGO computer games

Detailed animation and sound effects bring the world of trains to life

Build an aircraft with LEGO Creator, then watch it fly!

TERRIFIC TRAINS
Trains chuff along an endless supply of tracks, signals, and stations in LEGO Loco. The mail train even carries messages to LEGO Loco users around the world!

LEGO Media CD-ROMs focus on creativity, innovation, imagination, and fun

The Chess King, a collector's item included in the CD-ROM pack

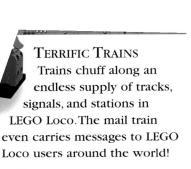

VIRTUAL CONSTRUCTION
With LEGO Creator, you can build all kinds of things, then go exploring inside your creations and watch them work. You can even destroy them with spectacular effects, then build them again using your instruction print-outs.

CHECK MATE
Anybody can be a champion with the CD-ROM game LEGO Chess. Ideal for beginners or experts, this is chess with a difference. Games are enacted by LEGO Mini figures; hilarious narration accompanies the action.

Biker Bob – LEGO Creator collector's item

Mini figures battle it out on the animated chess board. Both reds and blues have Indian brave pawns, backed up by Chiefs and Captains

Tunnel transporter

Giant drilling vehicle

16.67%   Doc: 9.87M/0K

ROCK RAIDERS TO THE RESCUE
Using hi-tech vehicles and equipment, Rock Raiders drill, dig, and blow up the rock underworld in order to excavate LEGO power crystals. They also encounter obstacles such as avalanches, volcanic lava, icy rivers – and hungry Rock Monsters!

ROCK RAIDERS RULE
A wild adventure game on CD-ROM, Rock Raiders involved much research and development. The game's authentic atmosphere was inspired by visiting mines in Scandinavia, and children tested the CD-ROM at each stage to ensure maximum excitement.

Docs – the geologist

Bandit – the helmsman

Axle – the driver

THE CURSE of the **MUMMY**
AN INTERACTIVE PUZZLE STORYBOOK

CASTLE MYSTERY
AN INTERACTIVE PUZZLE STORYBOOK

LEGO puzzle books require logic and intelligence

GOLD ROBBER

LEGO BOOKS
Books featuring popular sets and characters have joined the lines of licensed products. LEGO books are fun and educational; DUPLO books offer a complete learning program for preschool children, and older children can meet the challenge of the LEGO puzzle books, which feature 3-D graphics.

Sparks – the engineer

Jet – the pilot

BRICKS WITH CHIPS

I N THE AGE OF THE MICROCHIP, the LEGO Group developed a new generation of products that combined the LEGO Universe with the computer – and put a microchip into a LEGO brick. The result was the LEGO MINDSTORMS® Robotics Invention System. The aim was to inspire computer-literate children aged 10 years and up to make their toys literally come alive by giving them the chance to design, build, and program their very own working robots!

COSMIC BRAINWAVE
Launched in September 1998, LEGO MINDSTORMS introduced a world of robotic technology, "where the only limit is the power of the imagination."

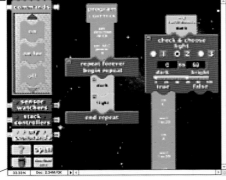

Light sensor

Touch sensor

Motor attached to an RCX microcomputer

LITTLE BRAIN
The brains of the LEGO MINDSTORMS System is the RCX brick – a microcomputer, which is programmable using a PC.

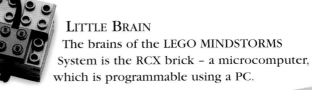

A CD-ROM provides the program and instructions for building various robots. Each robot can perform different tasks

LEGO MINDSTORMS has made the principles of robotics simple, but the possibilities are endless

The shape of future football players: ALF, the Advanced Logic Football roboid

Roboids search for minerals on asteroids

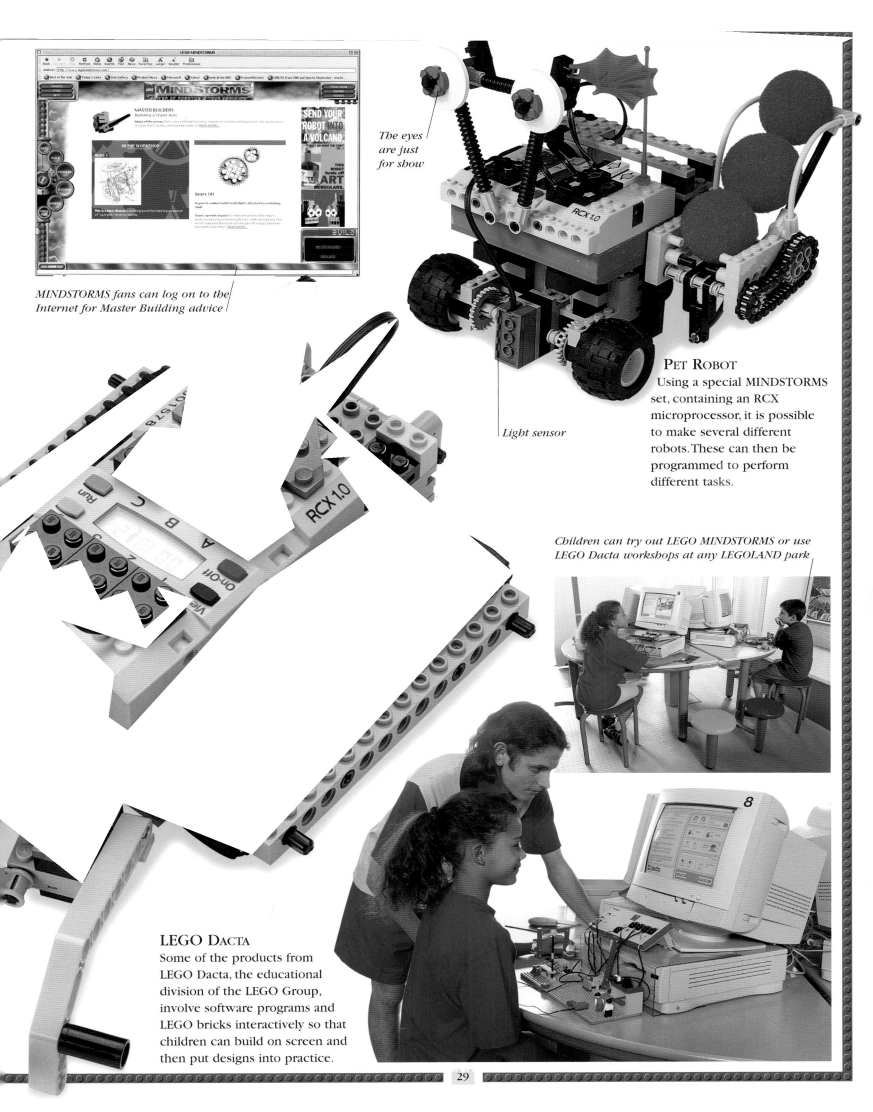

MINDSTORMS fans can log on to the Internet for Master Building advice

The eyes are just for show

Light sensor

PET ROBOT
Using a special MINDSTORMS set, containing an RCX microprocessor, it is possible to make several different robots. These can then be programmed to perform different tasks.

Children can try out LEGO MINDSTORMS or use LEGO Dacta workshops at any LEGOLAND park

LEGO DACTA
Some of the products from LEGO Dacta, the educational division of the LEGO Group, involve software programs and LEGO bricks interactively so that children can build on screen and then put designs into practice.

THE DESIGN CONCEPT

N EW LEGO CONCEPTS are conceived and then made real at a division called LEGO Futura. With offices all over the world, in Billund, Copenhagen, Milan, Tokyo, Boston, and London, LEGO Futura's staff are well placed to keep watch on, and gain inspiration from, scientific advances and trends in popular culture. All the designers in LEGO Futura take part in twice-yearly meetings, at which the LEGO Group's future products are presented and discussed.

An early form of Rock Raiders drill

As the Rock Raiders concept developed, the drill head became larger and metallic in appearance

BACK TO THE FUTURE
LEGO Futura's designers look for inspiration in the past as well as in the latest trends. For example, when creating a science fiction series such as Rock Raiders, they studied examples of old science fiction artwork (above).

This Rock Raiders component began as red, and ended up gray – a color more suited to the gritty feel of the product

Dramatic artwork creates an action-packed context for the Rock Raiders product line

A Rock Monster attacks a Rock Raiders drill

Background atmosphere helps stimulate creativity

EXPRESSING THE CONCEPT
Concept sketches such as the one above show the imaginative world a child enters when playing with the set. A written "universe description" fleshes out this world further, giving the set a background story, and each Mini figure a character.

A PROCESS OF EVOLUTION
Even the humblest items in a set may go through many stages. Not only must they be perfect, but the cost of producing them must be kept within limits.

The shape was also refined to ensure compatibility with other set elements

THE NEW WAY OF DESIGN
Computers are a vital part of the design process at LEGO Futura. The division also has a library of some 4,000 books for research purposes.

A Total Package

A new policy was adopted with the Rock Raiders series. The theme was developed in tandem with a CD-ROM game, shortly followed by a book. Each element "fed into" the other, helping to enrich the total concept.

The Rock Raiders exciting combination of hi-tech mining and sci-fi thrills is well suited to the set, game, and adventure story concepts

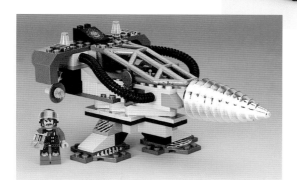

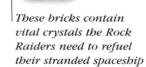

These bricks contain vital crystals the Rock Raiders need to refuel their stranded spaceship

Preparing the Plans

Twice a year, LEGO Futura design teams, above, present ideas to Group executives and marketing managers. The best concepts are developed further, then presented again. If a project looks promising, launch and marketing strategies are prepared.

Thinking Time

The Rock Raiders series of sets illustrated on these pages took eight months to develop. Some series take much longer – up to eight or nine years from first concept to finished product. Others are in the stores in just one and a half years.

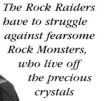

The Rock Raiders have to struggle against fearsome Rock Monsters, who live off the precious crystals

MAKING LEGO ELEMENTS

L EGO ELEMENTS BEGIN THEIR LIFE as tiny granules, which are produced in vast quantities and shipped to huge storage silos in LEGO factories. The Kornmarken factory in Billund has 14 silos, built to hold up to 33 tons (30 tonnes) of granules each! From these silos the granules are piped to giant, silent halls full of molding machines, which make them into elements.

THE BEGINNING
The 14 silos at the Kornmarken factory hold eight colors: blue, white, yellow, red, light gray, black (two silos each), dark gray, and green.

The silos are not usually filled to the top: a 33-ton (30-tonne) silo will probably hold up to 28 tons (26 tonnes) at a time

The granules are taken to the silos by truck and then sucked in via large hoses

From the silos, the granules are fed down pipes to the molding machines

The trucks are guided by grooves on the floor; they take full boxes to conveyor belts at the corner of the hall, and carry back empty boxes to the machines

The machines pour the newly molded LEGO pieces into boxes, collected by robot trucks

Radio and computer signals call the trucks to the machines when each box is full

THE LONELY ROBOT

The huge molding halls are almost empty. At Kornmarken two operators maintain 64 molding machines in each of the 12 molding halls, with help from maintenance technicians.

HOT AND COLD PLASTIC

Inside the molding machines, the granules are melted at 428–455°F (220–235°C). They are fed through to a mold and shaped to an accuracy of 0.005 mm. Then they are cooled and ejected, which takes seven to ten seconds.

The molding machine control panels are very sophisticated; they sense when a box is full, call the robot truck, continue making elements, but stop filling the full box until a new box arrives

The molds apply 27–165 tons (25–150 tonnes) of pressure, depending on the element being produced

At the end of the machine, the LEGO pieces may be dropped directly into boxes, or fed into them by mini-conveyor belts

There are not usually this many people present in real LEGO factories

STAGE TWO

THE NEWLY MOLDED LEGO pieces are taken to another LEGO factory to be finished off. Faces are printed on heads, decoration is put on machines and other elements. Arms and hands are added to torsos, heads to bodies, wheels to axles, tires to wheels, and the familiar LEGO elements emerge complete.

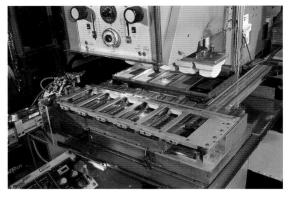

PAINT YOUR FACE?
The fine-tuned LEGO Groups's painting machines can apply multiple colors with complex patterns in a single operation. The tiny heads are gripped firmly in the decorating machines, which put paint on in a four-color pattern with a single, delicate stamp.

Workers unload the boxes of LEGO elements and take them to the machines

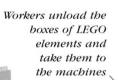

PEOPLE ZONE
Assembly halls are much less deserted than molding halls. There is, on average, one person per two machines, rather than one for every 32 machines.

In this example, axle units have the wheels and axles added and are put onto the conveyor belt at left

The LEGO pieces come from the molding factories in boxes

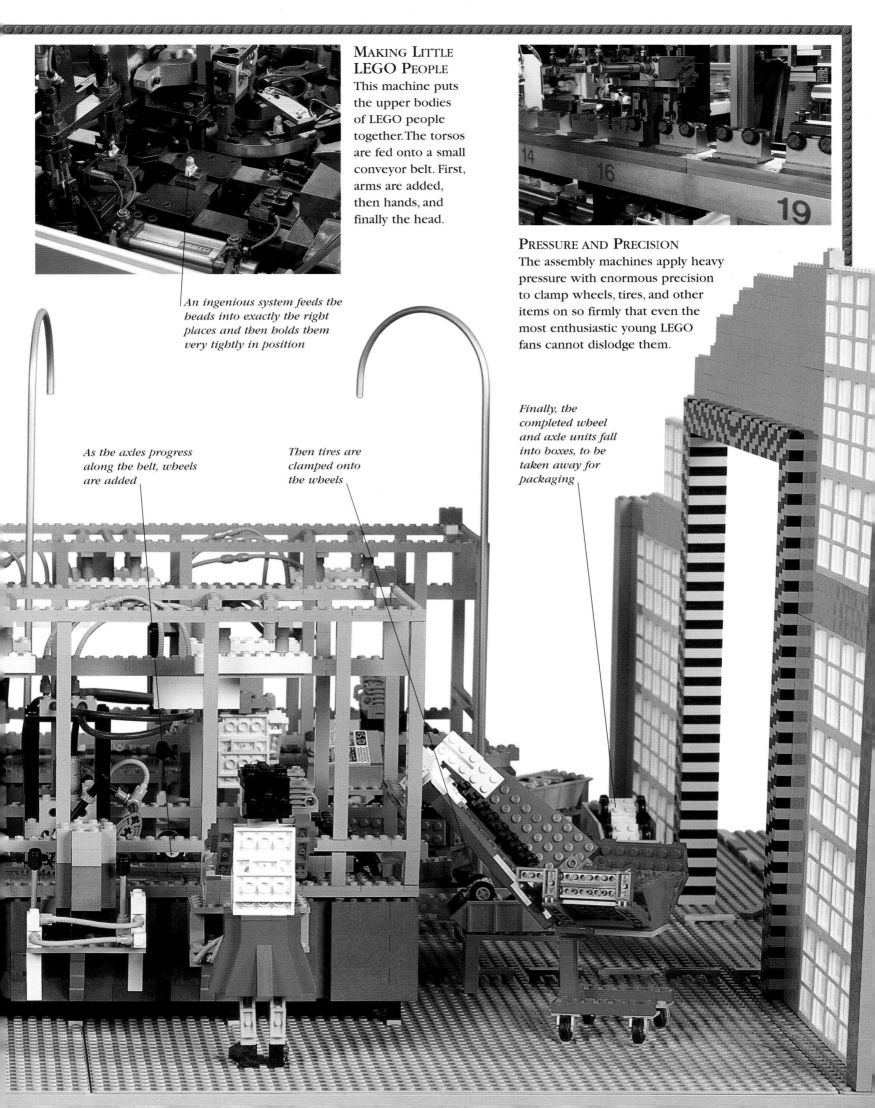

MAKING LITTLE LEGO PEOPLE

This machine puts the upper bodies of LEGO people together. The torsos are fed onto a small conveyor belt. First, arms are added, then hands, and finally the head.

An ingenious system feeds the heads into exactly the right places and then holds them very tightly in position

PRESSURE AND PRECISION

The assembly machines apply heavy pressure with enormous precision to clamp wheels, tires, and other items on so firmly that even the most enthusiastic young LEGO fans cannot dislodge them.

As the axles progress along the belt, wheels are added

Then tires are clamped onto the wheels

Finally, the completed wheel and axle units fall into boxes, to be taken away for packaging

14   16   19

AND FINALLY...

T HE LAST STAGE of production involves the packaging process. Some LEGO sets contain several hundred elements, so the packaging process has to work perfectly every time to avoid the dreaded "problem of the missing piece." The LEGO Group has invested heavily in special machinery made by LEGO Engineering in Billund, Denmark to solve this problem.

READY TO PACK
This operator's job is to feed elements into the vibrators, which sort them into different types, and also to ensure that the machine is running smoothly.

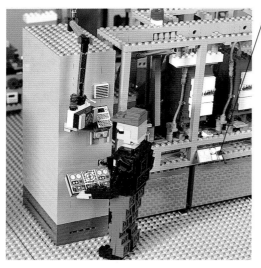

Control panel for operating the machine

THE CONTROLLER
This picture shows the other side of the packing machine, where the control panels are and where the controller stands.

Display trays (called inserts) are ready to be put onto pack conveyors

Element feeder

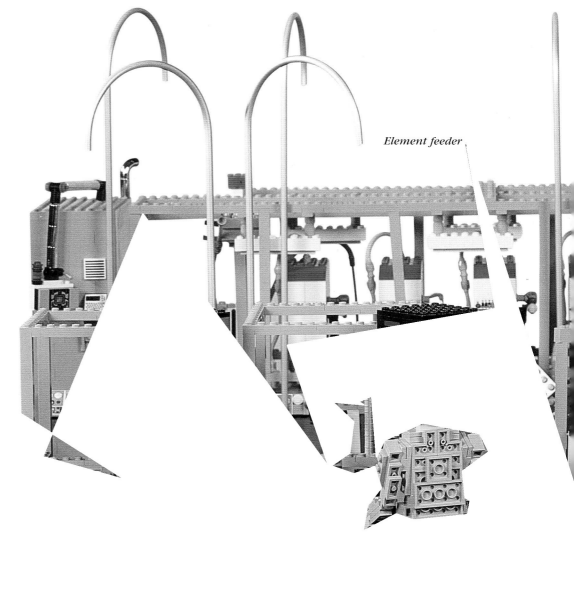

Display trays are loaded for transportation to final packing

LEGO SYSTEM
6585
6-10

THE FINAL TOUCH
This small LEGO box has been assembled after the elements have been counted, and the box erected and closed automatically on a packing line.

THE PACKAGING PROCESS
Boxes called cassettes move along a conveyor belt beneath bins. Each bin contains one type of element. As the cassette moves beneath the bin, the correct number and type of element drops into it. Meanwhile, packing operators fold the boxes, pack pieces, and watch out for any machine-made errors.

The packed display tray with LEGO elements

EASY-TO-SEE CONTENTS
The completed display tray is packed together with other LEGO elements into a large LEGO box. When the lid is opened, all the LEGO elements can be seen at a glance in the crystal-clear display tray.

Here, the final packed displays are checked visually by an operator

Five operators manually pack about 500 display trays per hour

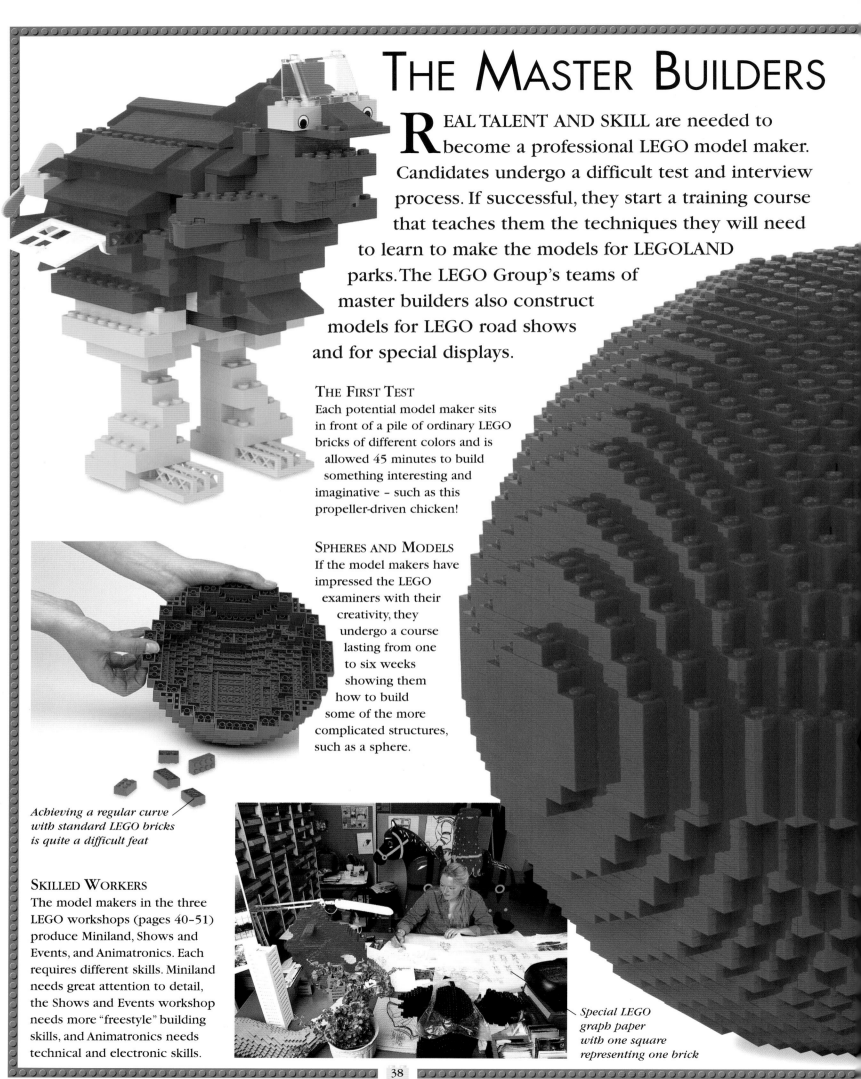

THE MASTER BUILDERS

REAL TALENT AND SKILL are needed to become a professional LEGO model maker. Candidates undergo a difficult test and interview process. If successful, they start a training course that teaches them the techniques they will need to learn to make the models for LEGOLAND parks. The LEGO Group's teams of master builders also construct models for LEGO road shows and for special displays.

THE FIRST TEST
Each potential model maker sits in front of a pile of ordinary LEGO bricks of different colors and is allowed 45 minutes to build something interesting and imaginative – such as this propeller-driven chicken!

SPHERES AND MODELS
If the model makers have impressed the LEGO examiners with their creativity, they undergo a course lasting from one to six weeks showing them how to build some of the more complicated structures, such as a sphere.

Achieving a regular curve with standard LEGO bricks is quite a difficult feat

SKILLED WORKERS
The model makers in the three LEGO workshops (pages 40–51) produce Miniland, Shows and Events, and Animatronics. Each requires different skills. Miniland needs great attention to detail, the Shows and Events workshop needs more "freestyle" building skills, and Animatronics needs technical and electronic skills.

Special LEGO graph paper with one square representing one brick

A LEGO MODEL MAKER AT WORK

Each model maker has a large desk surrounded by ranks of drawers containing LEGO bricks. Although LEGO elements are strong enough to stay connected, bricks are glued together so that the model can survive outdoor life and vigorous cleaning.

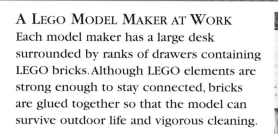

The model maker must be careful not to get glue on the outside of the model, or the bricks will lose color

Glue dispenser

Air extractor

Pliers

Rubber hammer

Metal pole supports body

PIECE BY PIECE

This model of a LEGO Friend is almost complete. The metal pole keeps it steady, supports the weight of the structure, and allows it to be moved safely.

The skills required to make a globe are used to make lifelike faces and heads

THE LEGO FRIEND

This is the completed LEGO Friend. The model will spend its life outdoors, so all its bricks have been glued together to make sure that they don't fall off or get "borrowed" by birds.

Each LEGO Friend has roughly 2,400 LEGO bricks and is about 2 ft 7 in (80 cm) tall

The two halves of the globe are made as mirror images of each other

LEGO Friends have wide feet to help keep them stable

THE PROFESSIONALS

O NCE THEY HAVE completed their training, LEGO model makers work in special workshops with millions of LEGO bricks at their disposal. They create the marvelous models that are seen in the LEGOLAND parks at Billund, Windsor, and Carlsbad. To build all the models for a LEGOLAND park takes about three years.

ELDER STATESMAN
This life-size head of Sir Winston Churchill, Britain's Prime Minister during World War II, was made by Darren Ward. He has captured the statesman in a typical pose.

PLANNING A FACE
Building a model's face is often the most difficult part of the process and can take a long time. Before construction starts, a detailed plan is made on special squared LEGO paper (see pages 60–61).

A half-size prototype is sometimes made to make sure that a model works

The giant blacksmith has a LEGO bandage on his thumb

CHECKING PROGRESS
As the model is being made, it is constantly checked against the original plans to ensure that no mistakes have been made.

Simple LEGO towers provide support while the model is being built

FINAL ASSEMBLY
The hands and head of a model are made separately and added to its body later. Model maker Darren Ward (right) is in the process of attaching one of the giant's hands.

FAMOUS FACES
Making a recognizable face of a famous personality is an extremely good test of a model maker's skill and ingenuity. The well-known faces on this page were all test pieces built at the Windsor Model Shop. They are superb examples of how simple LEGO bricks can be used in unexpected ways to produce brilliant results.

Heads such as this take between 30 and 40 hours to make

Luciano Pavarotti

Capturing the details around the eyes is often the key to a character

The techniques of building the helmet are similar to those used when making part of a sphere

Mr. Spock

The model maker has used an inventive combination of bricks to capture the character's tousled hair

The beard is made from roofing bricks

Herne the Hunter

Fred Flintstone

MODELSHOP BILLUND

THE LEGO GROUP runs three special model-making centers. Two provide the models for the Miniland parts of the parks, and the third constructs the models for the rest of the park areas. The oldest of the three is the Attraction Center at Billund. It was started in 1971 with 12 model designers, and now has 24 model designers and six animatronics experts, building ambitious models such as New York's Statue of Liberty, shown here.

MAIN STREET, MODEL TOWN
Model makers need flexible space in which to work. The main building is arranged around a central corridor big enough to take the models in and out. The tables can be moved and their height is easily adjusted. There are rows of drawers containing every LEGO element imaginable.

Each drawer contains a different LEGO piece and is labeled appropriately

The model is constructed around a central column for support

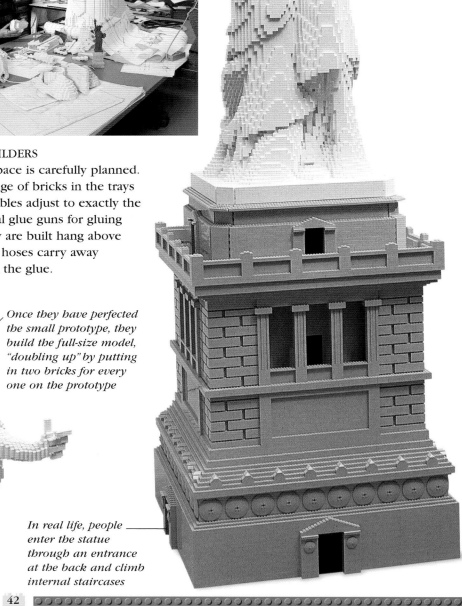

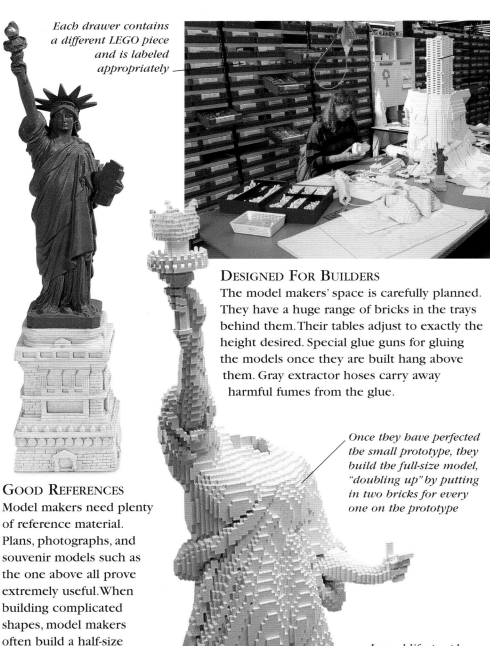

DESIGNED FOR BUILDERS
The model makers' space is carefully planned. They have a huge range of bricks in the trays behind them. Their tables adjust to exactly the height desired. Special glue guns for gluing the models once they are built hang above them. Gray extractor hoses carry away harmful fumes from the glue.

Once they have perfected the small prototype, they build the full-size model, "doubling up" by putting in two bricks for every one on the prototype

GOOD REFERENCES
Model makers need plenty of reference material. Plans, photographs, and souvenir models such as the one above all prove extremely useful. When building complicated shapes, model makers often build a half-size model first, because it is much easier to correct mistakes on a small model.

In real life, people enter the statue through an entrance at the back and climb internal staircases

Translucent bricks are used for the Statue of Liberty's torch to allow the light to shine through

A model designer (left) and animator (right) work together on the model

Viewing gallery lights in the statue's crown shine realistically

The model's head is able to bow in welcome

THE BILLUND TEAM

The creative team at Billund have created thousands of models. Every model is built using LEGO elements that are available in the stores (no cheating is allowed). The final versions are rebuilt with steel supports and extra-durable lights, to last for at least ten years.

The model weighs 418 lb (190 kg) and contains 12,200 LEGO bricks

BUILDING MT. RUSHMORE

F EATURING THE HEADS of four famous US presidents hewn from solid rock, Mount Rushmore, in South Dakota, is one of the most famous monuments in the US. A superb model of it, constructed from LEGO bricks by designers at Billund, is one of the main attractions of LEGOLAND California. The monument's original sculptor initially made a 1/12-scale model of each president's head before beginning work on the mountain. The LEGO model makers reversed this process – their model is 15 times smaller than the imposing original.

The model designers used brochures, photographs, and three-dimensional models like this souvenir as reference

THE BEGINNING
The designer begins by making sketches of the faces she is about to sculpt. Her drawing is so good that she can work out how to re-create the face in 3-D as she draws it.

This tool is used to press bricks firmly into place in awkward corners

The designer makes sure that the drawing and cross section match perfectly

HEAD START
The face of President Lincoln is gradually built up using a series of cross sections of the head made with LEGO bricks.

THE ORIGINAL

Mount Rushmore, South Dakota: Carved from the side of the mountain are giant busts of four of the most famous US presidents (from left), George Washington, Thomas Jefferson, Theodore Roosevelt, and Abraham Lincoln.

Most of the monument was sculpted by Gutzon Borglum between 1927 and 1941. His son finished it in 1955.

HEADS FIRST

Build on a scale of 1/15, each head took about 250 hours to make and used around 250,000 bricks. The presidents' hair was constructed separately. Great care was taken to capture facial expression.

George Washington's eyes blink while three little animated LEGO people clean his ear with a cotton swab!

Cotton swab moves in and out

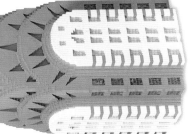

MODELSHOP WINDSOR

T HE SECOND LEGO model-making department is part of LEGOLAND Windsor and named the Models and Animation department. It was set up in 1993 to build models for the LEGOLAND parks. Around 20 model makers work there, in addition to designers and support staff. The Windsor team built half the Miniland models for the Windsor and LEGOLAND California parks and works on new projects for Miniland and for shows and rides.

BRIEF RECORD BREAKER
The 77-story Chrysler Building was the tallest building in the world when it was completed in 1930, but the Empire State Building overtook it the next year.

The design of the spire was inspired by features of Chrysler cars

SECRET SPIRE
The real spire was built in secret, to make sure that the Chrysler Building was taller than any rival.

GOING UP
The ground level of each building in Miniland is built at a scale of 1 to 20. Figures and cars are carefully built to scale.

INSIDE THE WORKSHOP
The desks of the Windsor model makers are ranged on either side of this wide central aisle. Extractor fans draw away the fumes of the glue used to afix the bricks of the models.

DESIGNING THE MODELS
The initial planning stage of a LEGO model entails visiting the building to photograph it from every angle and, if possible, acquiring blueprints and other detailed plans.

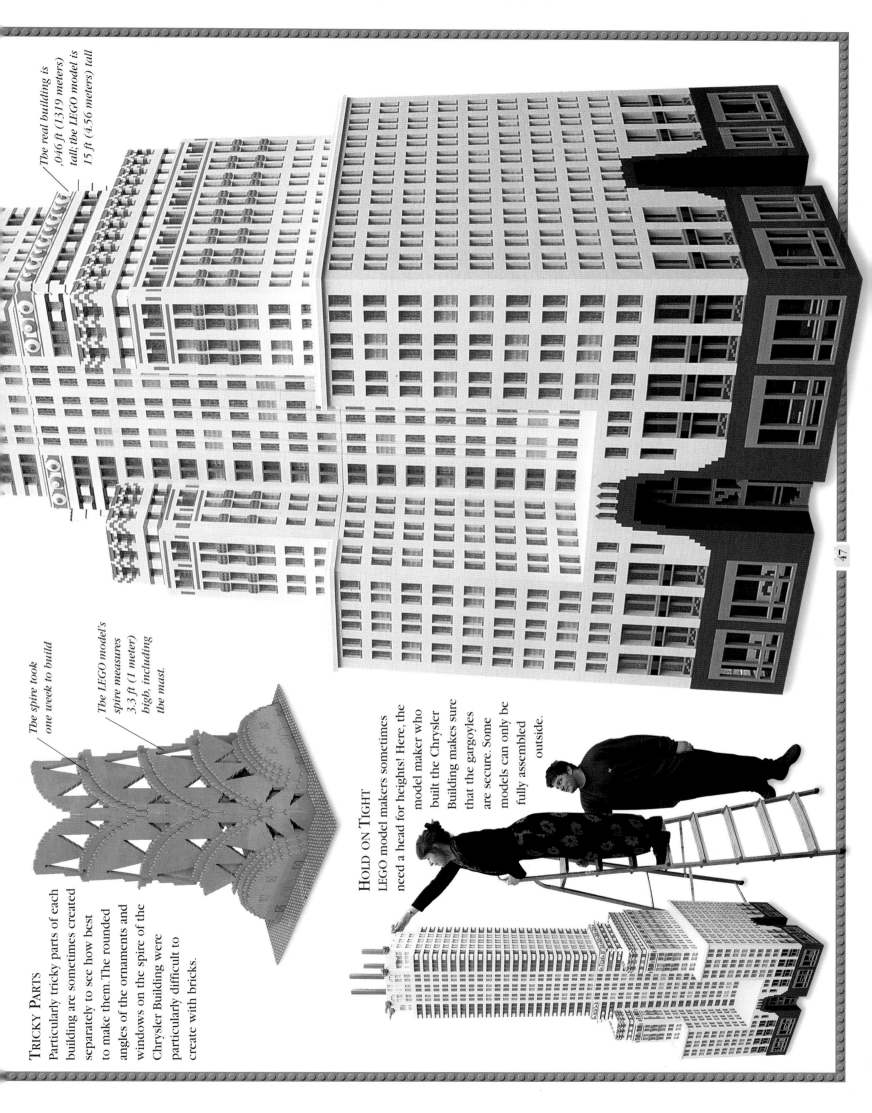

The real building is 1,046 ft (1319 meters) tall; the LEGO model is 15 ft (4.56 meters) tall

The spire took one week to build

The LEGO model's spire measures 3.3 ft (1 meter) high, including the mast.

Tricky Parts

Particularly tricky parts of each building are sometimes created separately to see how best to make them. The rounded angles of the ornaments and windows on the spire of the Chrysler Building were particularly difficult to create with bricks.

Hold on Tight

LEGO model makers sometimes need a head for heights! Here, the model maker who built the Chrysler Building makes sure that the gargoyles are secure. Some models can only be fully assembled outside.

GRAND CENTRAL STATION

ONE OF THE MOST INTRICATE constructions at Windsor is the model of Grand Central Station in New York City. The model in LEGOLAND California's Miniland contains 600,000 bricks and took four model makers six months to build. The model-making team faced an unusual challenge: this structure had to be cut away so that visitors to the park could see the different levels and spaces inside.

NEW YORK LANDMARK
Situated on 42nd Street, the real station was opened in 1913. More than half a million people pass through it every day.

PHOTOGRAPHS OF THE SITE
Before any modeling can start, the model maker will often go to see the building to be built and take a large number of photographs for reference. This is important because books rarely show enough detail.

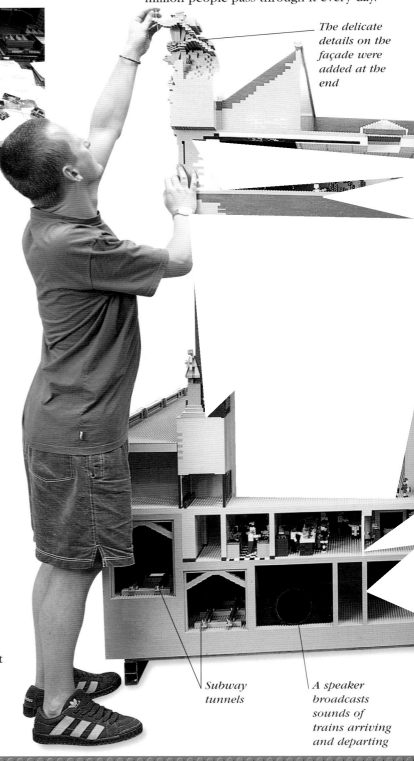

The delicate details on the façade were added at the end

STARTING THE MODEL
On a model the size of Grand Central Station there is more than one model maker, and animators will be responsible for providing the moving parts. The first layers of bricks act as the foundations of the model, and must be carefully placed – any mistakes made at this stage would take a long time to undo if discovered after the model is finished.

The diner

LUNCH BREAK
While the model was being built, a lot of effort went into making sure that there were eye-catching scenes, like these subway tunnels and the diner.

Subway tunnels

A speaker broadcasts sounds of trains arriving and departing

A line of schoolchildren is supervised by their teacher

BUSY BUILDING
This LEGO Grand Central Station model is most unusual – not many train stations have tennis courts and an art gallery!

The station's information board

Information booth

MAIN STATION CONCOURSE
The massive roof of the main concourse took 80 hours to make and used 30,000 LEGO bricks. Each figure uses roughly 50 bricks. Elevators full of passengers rise and descend, and escalators smoothly carry people from floor to floor.

The chandeliers are lit using fiber-optic cable

A speaker in the roof broadcasts sound effects of crowd noise

HUSTLE AND BUSTLE
It is important for model makers to get the "feel" of a place right, as well as the architectural details. Stations are busy places with a great deal of activity and a wide range of people. This scene features a guide dog, ticket booths, and a luggage cart.

New York city police

SHOWS AND EVENTS

THE LEGO GROUP'S third model-making division is the Shows and Events department at Billund. When a new LEGO line is launched or a major LEGO company event is held, the Shows and Events team swings into action to build spectacular promotional models. They specialize in fun and fantasy and in creating humorous, appealing characters.

THE MODEL MAKERS
The Shows and Events department was established in 1989 to construct special models that could be used to raise the LEGO Group's public profile. The department, which has 19 designers, constructs more than 200 models for various events each year.

The Shows and Events team are experts at giving life and humor to their models

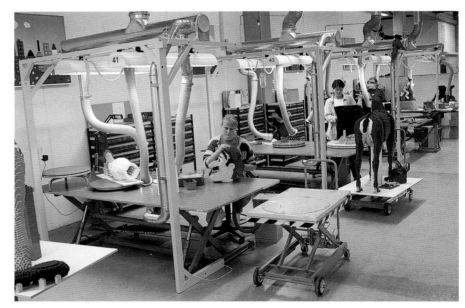

Equipment on models is designed to work as realistically as possible

HEAVY DUTY
This breakdown truck, called a Kenworth Heavy Duty Wrecker, took nearly 50 hours to build, weighs nearly 4 lb 8 oz (2 kg), and contains about 2,000 bricks. The cable car (right) was built for San Francisco Miniland at LEGOLAND California. It contains about 2,600 bricks.

PARTY TIME!

LEGO designers know how to have fun. One party at the department saw the Yellow Submarine, being created for LEGOLAND California (see page 94), swathed in Danish flags after a Danish victory in the 1998 soccer World Cup.

This is Danish for "congratulations"

The pattern on the beefeater's uniform was carefully worked out on paper before building started

There are now 12 different Ollies at the LEGOLAND parks, Shows and Events, and elsewhere

ON PARADE

This Beefeater was created for a display in Hamley's toy shop, London, in 1996. The theme was Tourism in London.

This version of Ollie took 15 hours to build and contains 1,162 bricks

Ollie is now a popular fixture at the LEGO parks and is the hero of the Castle Mystery book

THE FRIENDLY DRAGON

Shows and Events created Ollie, a friendly, cheerful dragon, to promote the Castle series. He was part of several life-size scenes that the department built to celebrate the set's exciting "sword and sorcery" world. Similar shows on other themes are mounted at large toy shops in many countries.

IMAGINATION RULES

BECAUSE THEY SPECIALIZE in building imaginary creatures, the Shows and Events department have to create their own reference material. Before they start building with LEGO bricks, they construct little clay models to judge how the design will look in three dimensions. They then proceed in the same way as the model makers at the Attraction Centers, building half-size models of difficult shapes, then "doubling up" the bricks for the real thing.

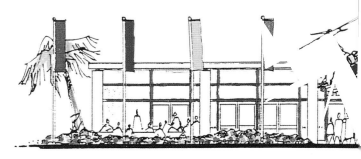

HOW THE SITE WILL LOOK
Huge, brightly colored LEGO structures will dominate this entrance to the Imagination Center in LEGOLAND, California. There are decorative palm trees, a flying machine is hovering high up, a family of giraffes grazes, and there's an enormous ice-cream cone. These create an impression of fun and adventure, and also tempt visitors young and old alike to try the activities within.

MAKING SCALE MODELS
The model maker scales up a small clay figure to create a half-size version. The Attraction Centers rarely do this; it is common practice for Shows and Events.

The clay kangaroo is painted, so the overall impact of the final model can be assessed

The larger of these two models now reclines in the DUPLO shop at LEGOLAND California

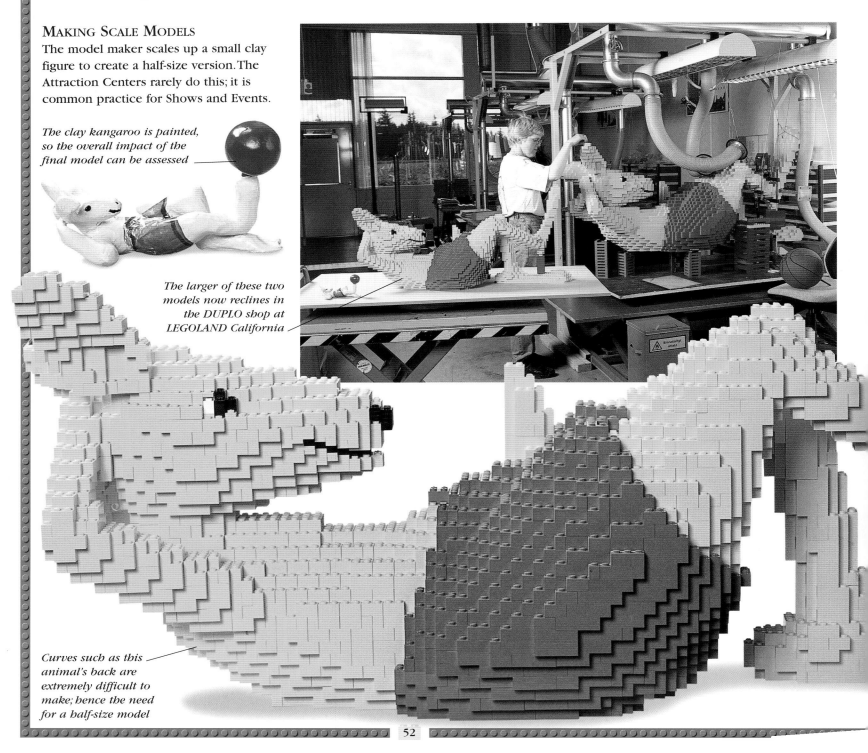

Curves such as this animal's back are extremely difficult to make; hence the need for a half-size model

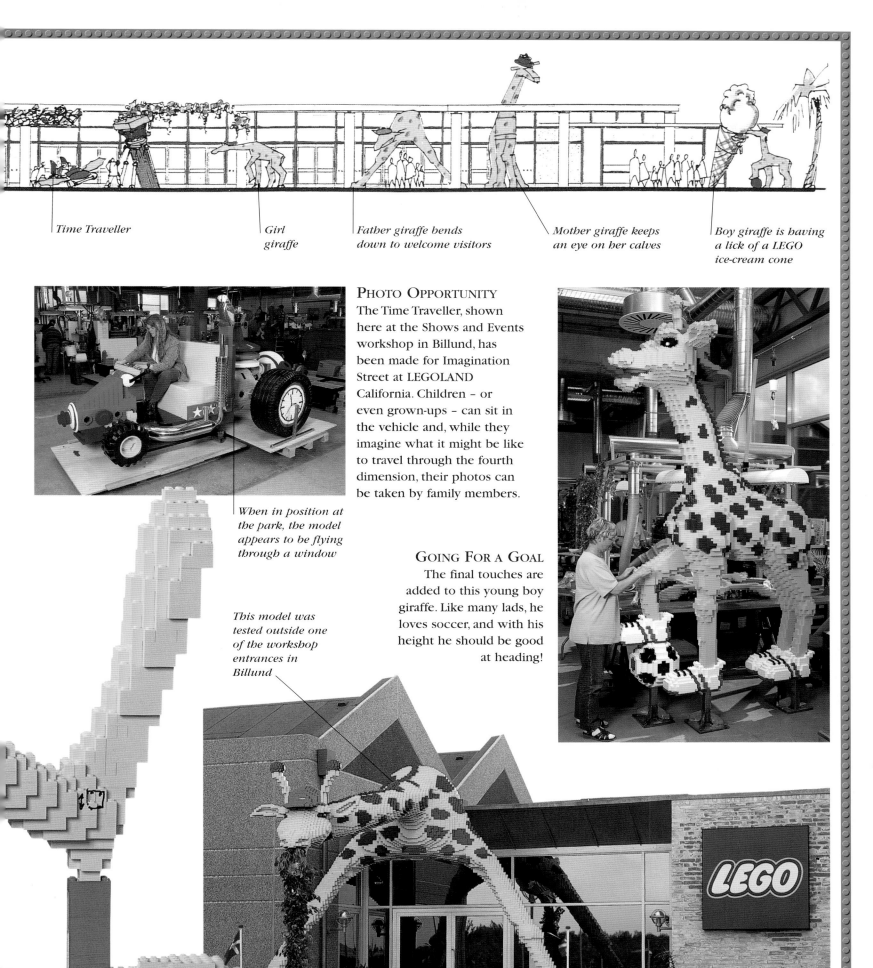

Time Traveller

Girl giraffe

Father giraffe bends down to welcome visitors

Mother giraffe keeps an eye on her calves

Boy giraffe is having a lick of a LEGO ice-cream cone

PHOTO OPPORTUNITY

The Time Traveller, shown here at the Shows and Events workshop in Billund, has been made for Imagination Street at LEGOLAND California. Children – or even grown-ups – can sit in the vehicle and, while they imagine what it might be like to travel through the fourth dimension, their photos can be taken by family members.

When in position at the park, the model appears to be flying through a window

This model was tested outside one of the workshop entrances in Billund

GOING FOR A GOAL

The final touches are added to this young boy giraffe. Like many lads, he loves soccer, and with his height he should be good at heading!

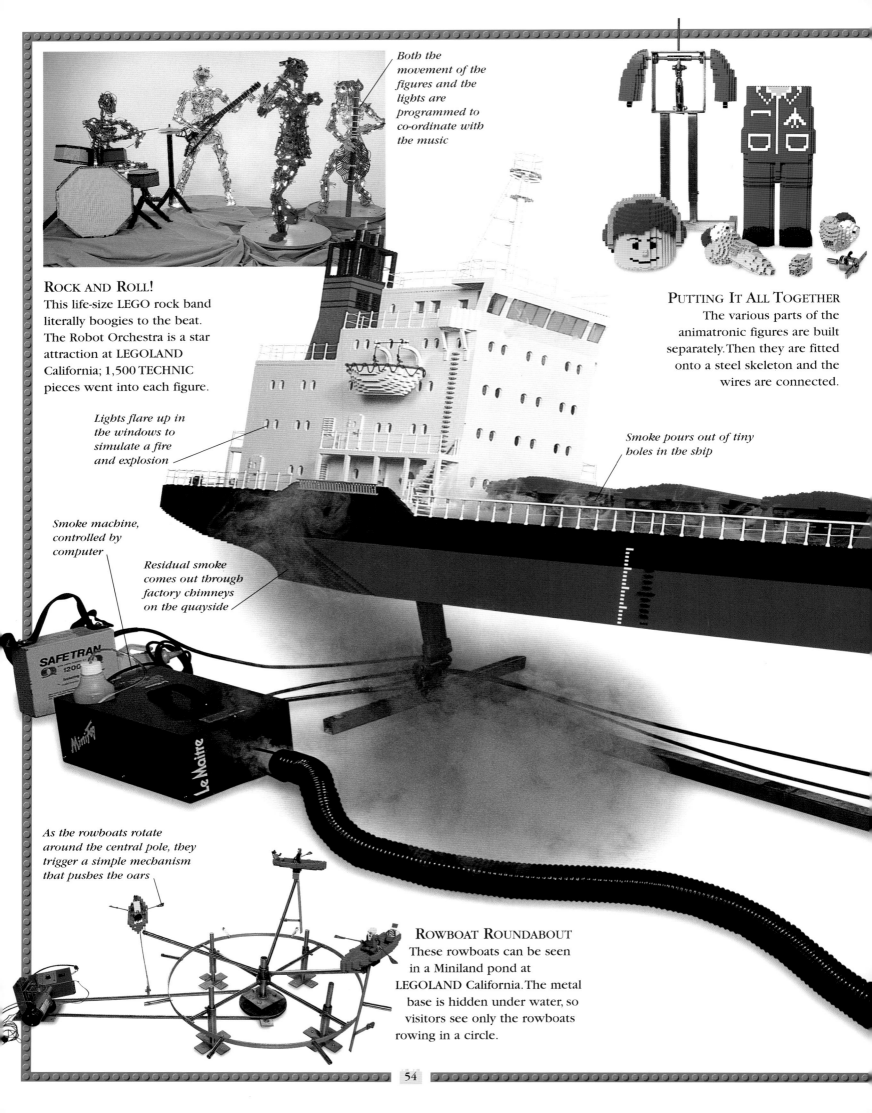

ROCK AND ROLL!

This life-size LEGO rock band literally boogies to the beat. The Robot Orchestra is a star attraction at LEGOLAND California; 1,500 TECHNIC pieces went into each figure.

Both the movement of the figures and the lights are programmed to co-ordinate with the music

PUTTING IT ALL TOGETHER

The various parts of the animatronic figures are built separately. Then they are fitted onto a steel skeleton and the wires are connected.

Lights flare up in the windows to simulate a fire and explosion

Smoke pours out of tiny holes in the ship

Smoke machine, controlled by computer

Residual smoke comes out through factory chimneys on the quayside

As the rowboats rotate around the central pole, they trigger a simple mechanism that pushes the oars

ROWBOAT ROUNDABOUT

These rowboats can be seen in a Miniland pond at LEGOLAND California. The metal base is hidden under water, so visitors see only the rowboats rowing in a circle.

ANIMATRONICS

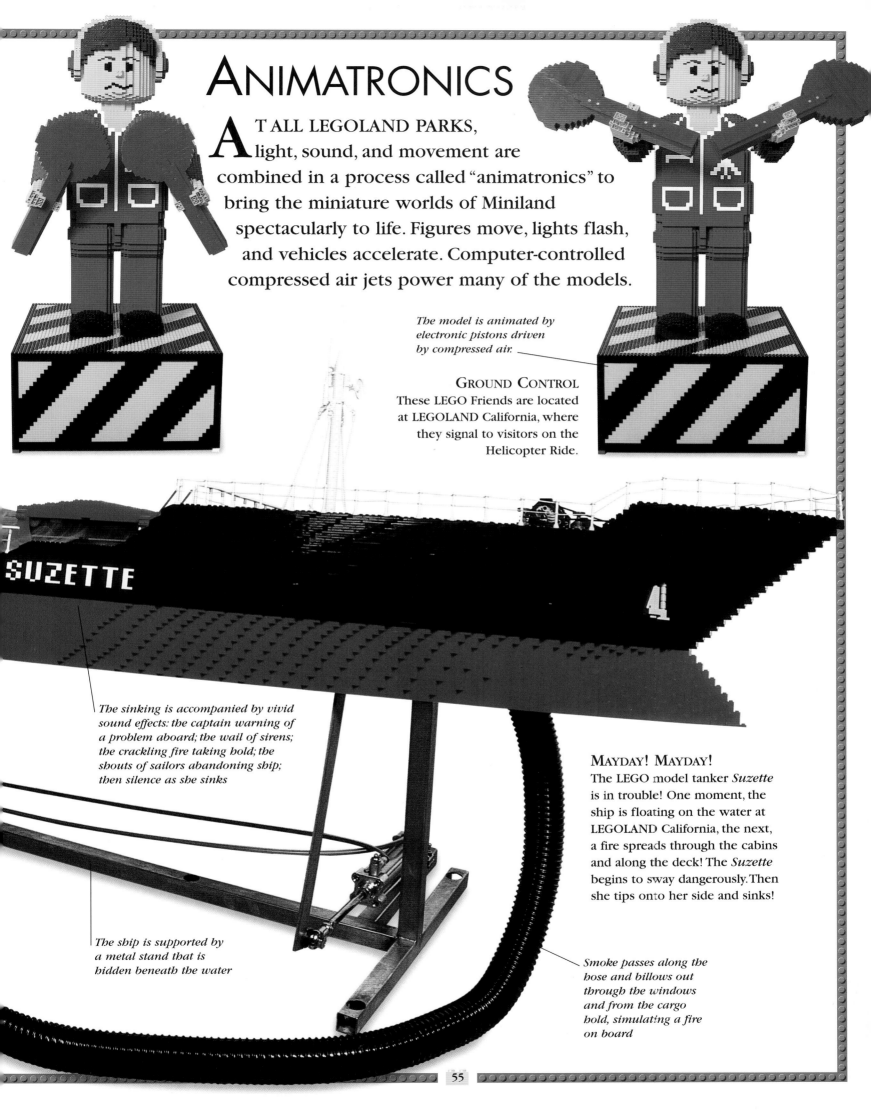

AT ALL LEGOLAND PARKS, light, sound, and movement are combined in a process called "animatronics" to bring the miniature worlds of Miniland spectacularly to life. Figures move, lights flash, and vehicles accelerate. Computer-controlled compressed air jets power many of the models.

The model is animated by electronic pistons driven by compressed air.

GROUND CONTROL
These LEGO Friends are located at LEGOLAND California, where they signal to visitors on the Helicopter Ride.

The sinking is accompanied by vivid sound effects: the captain warning of a problem aboard; the wail of sirens; the crackling fire taking hold; the shouts of sailors abandoning ship; then silence as she sinks

MAYDAY! MAYDAY!
The LEGO model tanker *Suzette* is in trouble! One moment, the ship is floating on the water at LEGOLAND California, the next, a fire spreads through the cabins and along the deck! The *Suzette* begins to sway dangerously. Then she tips onto her side and sinks!

The ship is supported by a metal stand that is hidden beneath the water

Smoke passes along the hose and billows out through the windows and from the cargo hold, simulating a fire on board

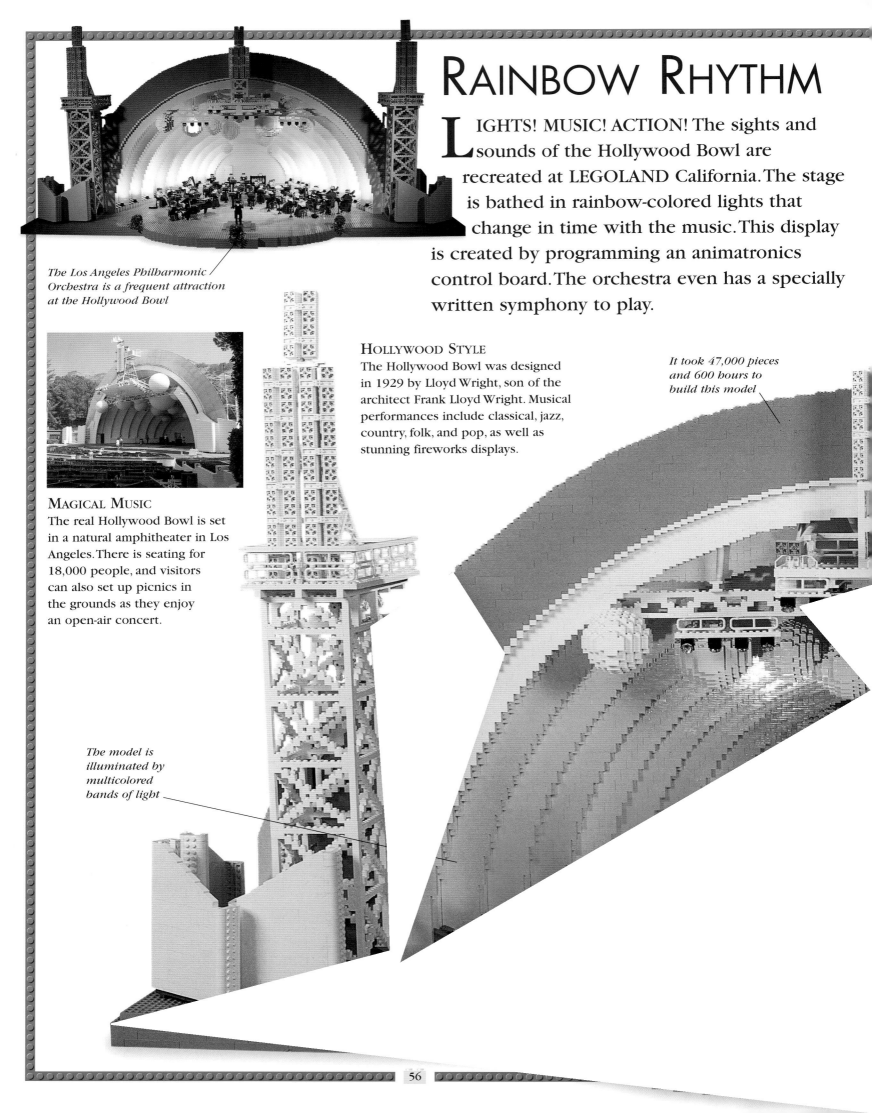

Rainbow Rhythm

LIGHTS! MUSIC! ACTION! The sights and sounds of the Hollywood Bowl are recreated at LEGOLAND California. The stage is bathed in rainbow-colored lights that change in time with the music. This display is created by programming an animatronics control board. The orchestra even has a specially written symphony to play.

The Los Angeles Philharmonic Orchestra is a frequent attraction at the Hollywood Bowl

HOLLYWOOD STYLE
The Hollywood Bowl was designed in 1929 by Lloyd Wright, son of the architect Frank Lloyd Wright. Musical performances include classical, jazz, country, folk, and pop, as well as stunning fireworks displays.

It took 47,000 pieces and 600 hours to build this model

MAGICAL MUSIC
The real Hollywood Bowl is set in a natural amphitheater in Los Angeles. There is seating for 18,000 people, and visitors can also set up picnics in the grounds as they enjoy an open-air concert.

The model is illuminated by multicolored bands of light

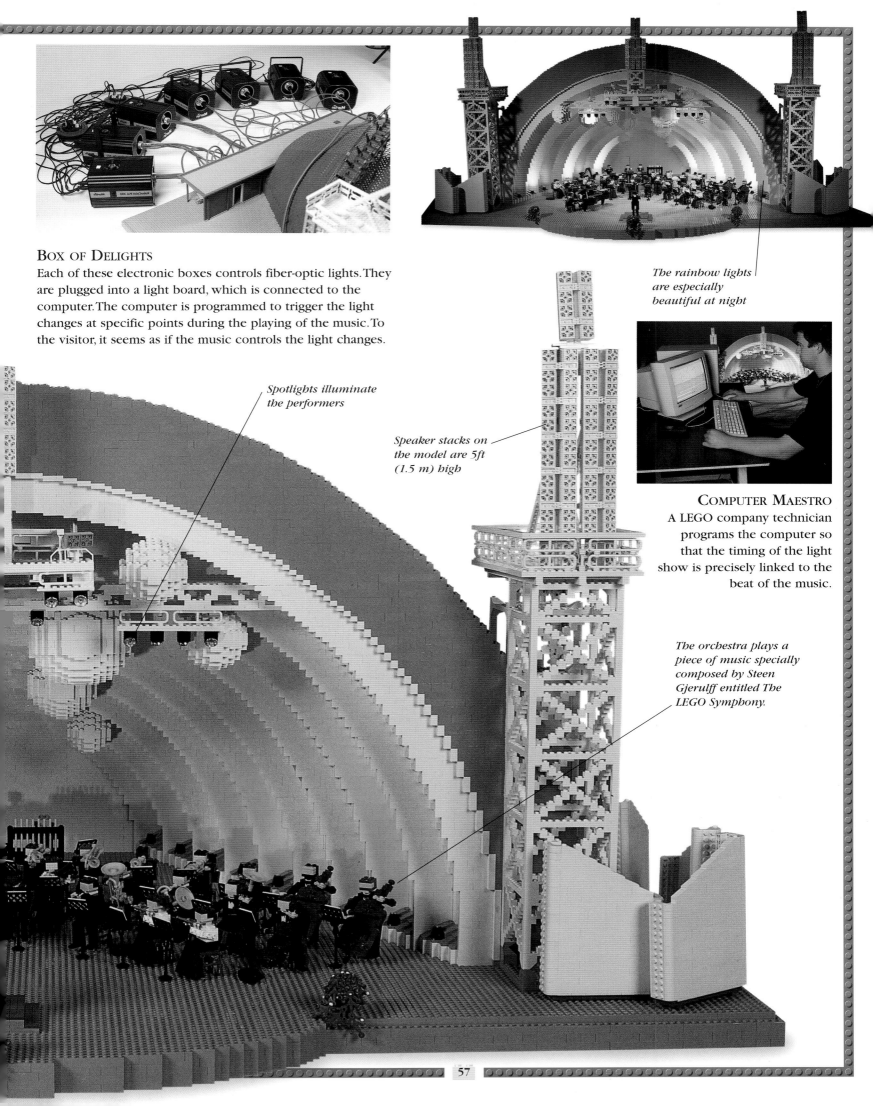

BOX OF DELIGHTS

Each of these electronic boxes controls fiber-optic lights. They are plugged into a light board, which is connected to the computer. The computer is programmed to trigger the light changes at specific points during the playing of the music. To the visitor, it seems as if the music controls the light changes.

The rainbow lights are especially beautiful at night

Spotlights illuminate the performers

Speaker stacks on the model are 5ft (1.5 m) high

COMPUTER MAESTRO

A LEGO company technician programs the computer so that the timing of the light show is precisely linked to the beat of the music.

The orchestra plays a piece of music specially composed by Steen Gjerulff entitled The LEGO Symphony.

ART OF ILLUSION

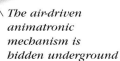

T HE LEGO MODEL MAKERS' attention to detail is so acute that they even take account of the angle from which their models will be viewed. This Miniland cafeteria is designed to be viewed from only one angle, so only one side has a finished interior.

NEW ORLEANS NIGHTLIFE
This LEGO model of the Bourbon Café is part of the New Orleans Miniland exhibit at LEGOLAND California. The model shows a busy night at the café, with lots of people and action.

SPIN YOUR PARTNER
At LEGOLAND California the band plays rousing country music on the back of a hay wagon. The musicians actually "play" their instruments with the help of animatronics.

The air-driven animatronic mechanism is hidden underground

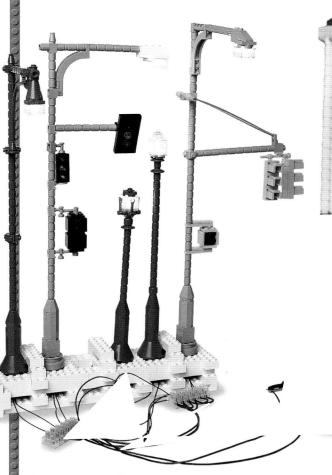

STREETLIGHT SERENADE
Realistic details in Miniland include traffic lights and streetlights. Different styles are made to suit every location. This is an assortment of lights for an American street.

The model includes waiters with trays and dishes on the tables

TAKING THE LID OFF
Behind the clever façade of this building, intricate wiring allows the designers to create natural-looking light and shadows. People and furniture are placed precisely so that they are clearly seen through the windows. This creates an illusion of a busy café, although in reality, much of the building is filled with electronic panels.

A café customer takes a breath of fresh air

Electronic control panels are hidden inside these boxes

Model makers used 23,000 pieces to build the Bourbon Café

Lights flicker inside, adding to the illusion

Open doors allow visitors to glimpse the inside of the café

DESIGNING ON PAPER

PLANNING IS THE KEY to building complex objects with LEGO bricks. Professional model makers begin by sketching the object on special paper that is marked out in squares, much like graph paper. With their preliminary sketches they create the basic look of the object from different points of view. Then they alter the line of the sketches to match the squares on the paper. Each square represents one LEGO brick. The model makers now have a plan to use as a guide.

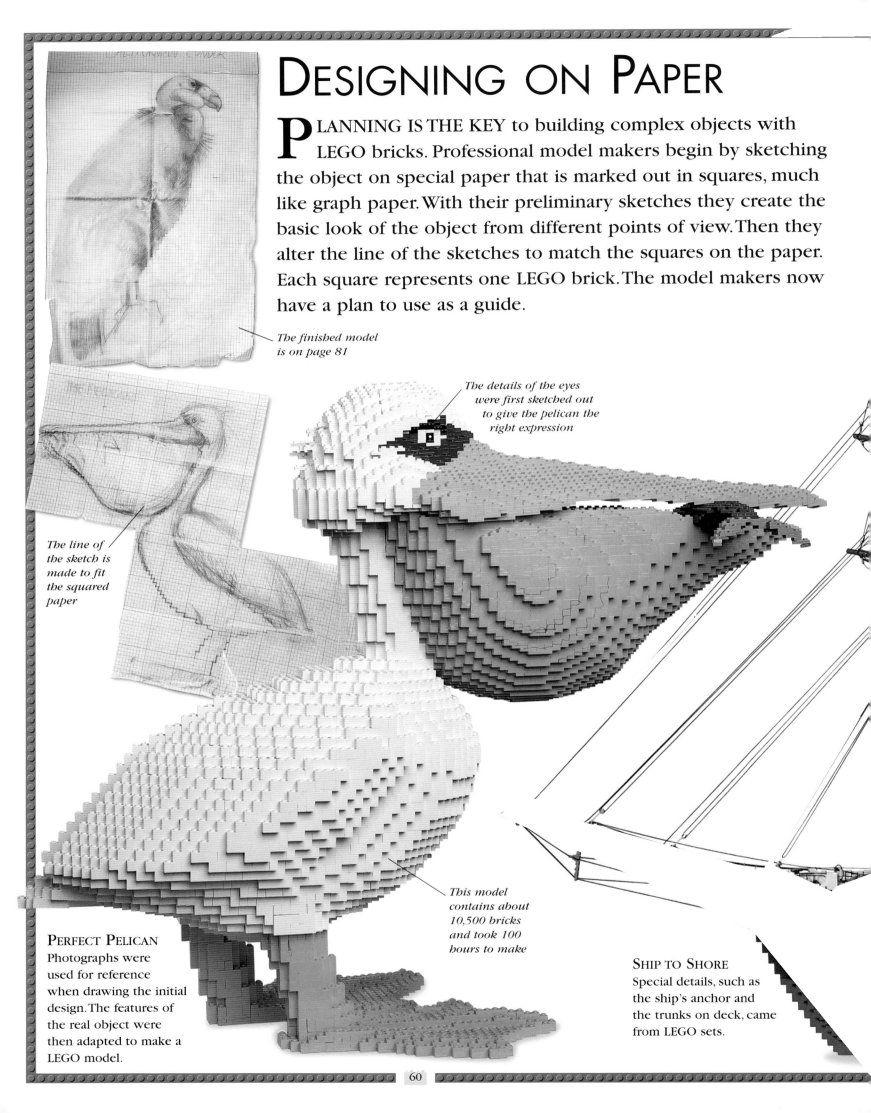

The finished model is on page 81

The details of the eyes were first sketched out to give the pelican the right expression

The line of the sketch is made to fit the squared paper

PERFECT PELICAN
Photographs were used for reference when drawing the initial design. The features of the real object were then adapted to make a LEGO model.

This model contains about 10,500 bricks and took 100 hours to make

SHIP TO SHORE
Special details, such as the ship's anchor and the trunks on deck, came from LEGO sets.

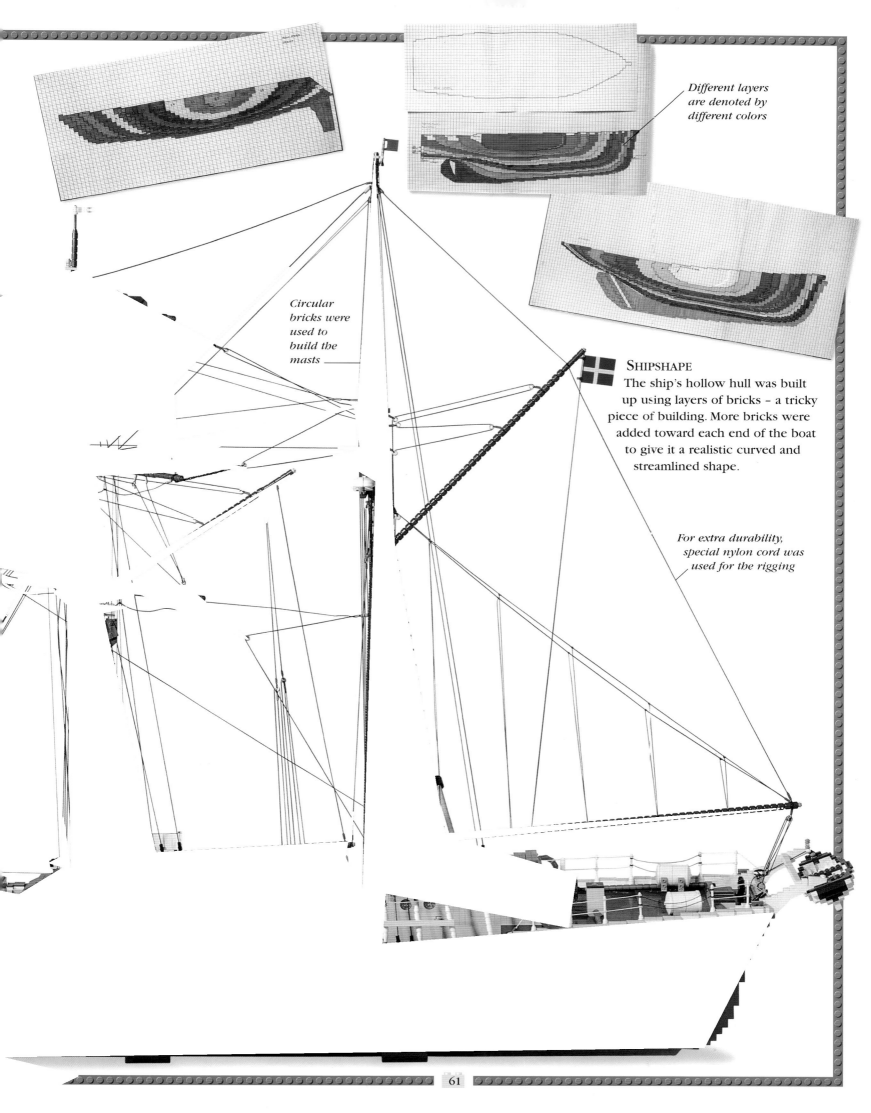

*Different layers
are denoted by
different colors*

*Circular
bricks were
used to
build the
masts*

SHIPSHAPE

The ship's hollow hull was built
up using layers of bricks – a tricky
piece of building. More bricks were
added toward each end of the boat
to give it a realistic curved and
streamlined shape.

*For extra durability,
special nylon cord was
used for the rigging*

LEGO LETTERING

NAMES AND TITLES make your models more personal. With careful planning, you can incorporate lettering into your LEGO models. As when designing other complicated shapes, use grid paper to draw the letters so you will know which pieces to use, and where to place them to form each letter. Build sample lettering first, then add it in as you build the rest of the model, using your grid as a guide.

NORTH, SOUTH, EAST, OR WEST?
You can make directions such as "East" (above), or road signs or even mosaic artworks, a part of your models.

Make sample letters to see whether your plan works

Draw the LEGO letters on the grid; when building your model, use the grid as a guide for lettering

ALL ABOARD!
Model makers put the final touches to this car ferry. The ferry's name, "Rowan," is planned in advance and built in as the model progresses.

CITY SANCTUARY
This Manhattan building from the LEGOLAND California Miniland features real New York-style graffiti. Having created the colorful spray-can-style mural on the outside walls, the modeler added his name in "street-art" lettering, just like a real graffiti artist. A rooftop gym – a typical feature in space-starved Manhattan – completes the building.

The modeler's signature in "street-art" style

BUILDING BOOKS

A simple way to experiment with lettering is to make a LEGO book. We've used word play here to make our own versions of popular classics.

The grid shows which pieces to use and where to place them to make letters

Smooth brick

The title slots in, without a stud connection

Experiment with different styles of lettering

STYLISH LETTERS

Try experimenting with different LEGO pieces. Block lettering is easiest, but curved lettering can look more stylish.

A LITERARY LEGO IDEA

Make your own library of LEGO books. You can design different lettering and decorations for each cover – and make up your own puns, too! If you're really ambitious, you can write a whole page or poem in LEGO letters!

This decoration mimics the look of leather-bound classic books

BUILDING LITTLE PEOPLE

H AVE YOU EVER MADE your own cast of LEGO characters? These figures were made by LEGO model makers. You can see some of them at LEGOLAND parks. LEGO Mini figures are 4 in (10 cm) high and populate Minilands, in scale with the buildings. LEGO Friends are about 3 ft (80 cm) tall, the height of a young child, and are in parts of the parks. Some are animated.

The figure is 15 in (36 cm) high

Lucky, the LEGO puppy, learns some new tricks

SURPRISE!

This chap is a caricature of a former President of the LEGO Club, Clive Nicholls. It was given to him on his last day of work as a gift by his colleagues at Windsor.

Watch out for this lobster's claws!

Use roofing bricks at the bottom of the legs for groovy flares

Position the arms behind the shoulder, ready to swing

GOLF, ANYONE?

You can just imagine these sporting figures on the golf course.

Cross the legs for a relaxed stance while waiting to tee off

LEGO Lenny's dog takes him for a walk. Look out, Lenny!

The blushing bride

Lisa and Larry tie the knot

Lulu trains her new puppy

Parents take their babies for a stroll in the park

"Say cheese!" Holiday snaps at the beach

A big sister takes her brother to school. "Hurry, or we'll be late!"

But little brother has mischief on his mind ...

This metal prop will later be made to look like a fireman's hose

FRIENDLY FIREFIGHTER This LEGO Friend was made for LEGOLAND California. In real life, he is eight times the size of the Minifigures on the rest of the page.

Use lots of small LEGO pieces to make everyday machines such as this lawnmower

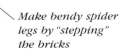

HOW TO MAKE IT

THERE IS NO RIGHT WAY to make something with LEGO bricks – the right way is whatever way you choose. Learning from others' ideas can help. On the next few pages we show some of the off-duty creations of professional LEGO model makers. We hope they inspire you to new heights of creativity!

Make bendy spider legs by "stepping" the bricks

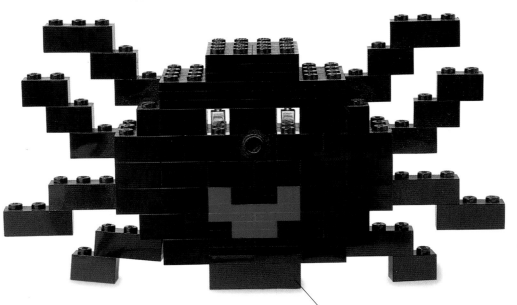

Start with the basic shape, then add things such as legs etc.

Sections of LEGO chain link are easy to make and have many uses

A curvy Conga-style line adds interest

Use a bright LEGO coaster under your next cup of coffee

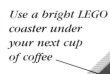

You can extend the spiral at the end, the top, or the sides

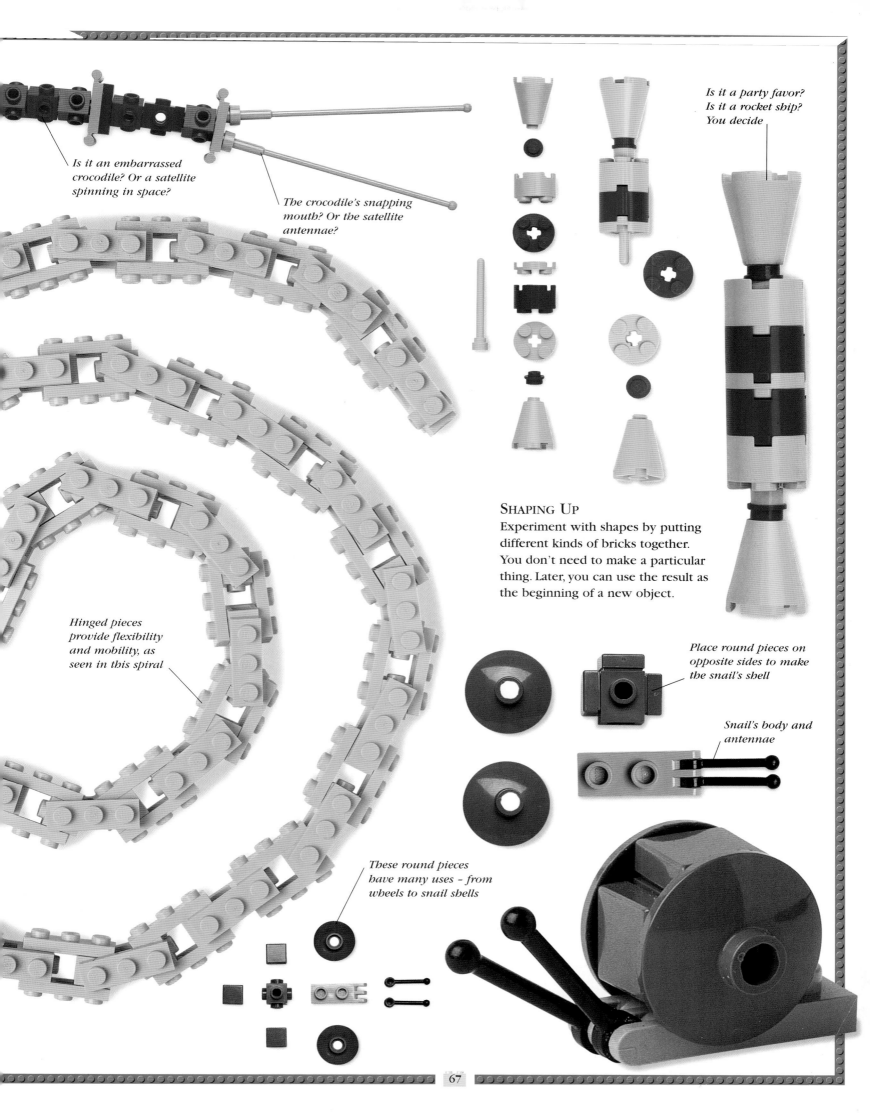

Is it an embarrassed crocodile? Or a satellite spinning in space?

The crocodile's snapping mouth? Or the satellite antennae?

Is it a party favor? Is it a rocket ship? You decide

SHAPING UP
Experiment with shapes by putting different kinds of bricks together. You don't need to make a particular thing. Later, you can use the result as the beginning of a new object.

Hinged pieces provide flexibility and mobility, as seen in this spiral

Place round pieces on opposite sides to make the snail's shell

Snail's body and antennae

These round pieces have many uses - from wheels to snail shells

CREATIVE PLAY

The creative challenge of using LEGO elements is to adapt the bricks and pieces at your disposal to your needs. The overall effect is more important than being precise, so try to be as flexible in your thinking as possible. For example, you may be surprised how many different sorts of bricks can be used to suggest a human hand or how many ways you can make pieces of your models move realistically.

Small pieces make handy connectors

The finished duck

The bricks used for this dog are standard LEGO bricks

Different-colored bricks convey the shades of the duck's plumage

A small LEGO hinge allows Elvis's shoulder to move

A bright band of color suggests Elvis's silk cummerbund

A piece of string is ideal for Elvis's microphone cord

Hinged pieces allow the paws to move

Add an extra LEGO piece to the dog's face for its cold, wet nose

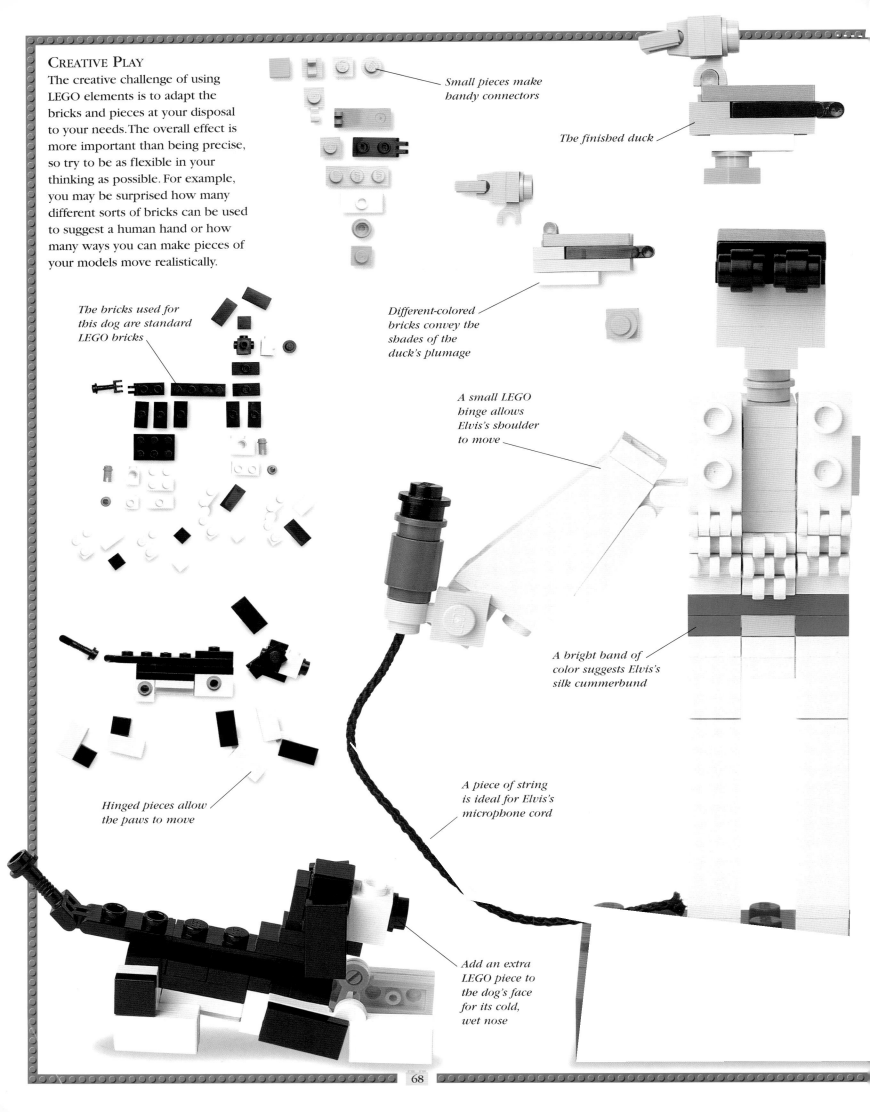

IMAGINATION STRETCHERS

LEGO ELEMENTS ARE BUILDING tools that really stretch the imagination. Once you know the basics, you can make just about anything! Perhaps some of the ideas shown here may help to inspire your own unique creations.

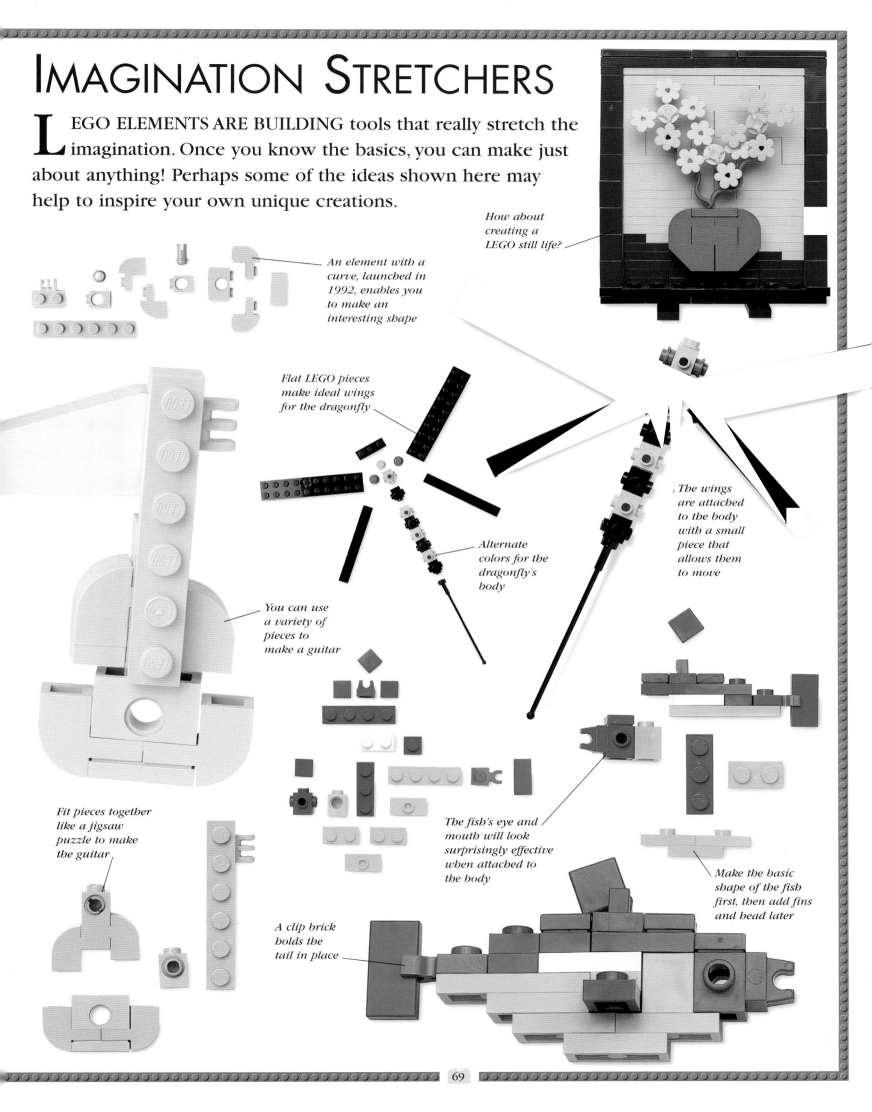

How about creating a LEGO still life?

An element with a curve, launched in 1992, enables you to make an interesting shape

Flat LEGO pieces make ideal wings for the dragonfly

The wings are attached to the body with a small piece that allows them to move

Alternate colors for the dragonfly's body

You can use a variety of pieces to make a guitar

Fit pieces together like a jigsaw puzzle to make the guitar

The fish's eye and mouth will look surprisingly effective when attached to the body

Make the basic shape of the fish first, then add fins and head later

A clip brick holds the tail in place

ENDLESS INVENTIONS

WITH A LITTLE INGENUITY you can make all kinds of things with LEGO pieces, from everyday objects to extraordinary characters, without needing to use a lot of bricks. Because all LEGO pieces have a variety of uses and can be attached in different ways, the possibilities are literally endless!

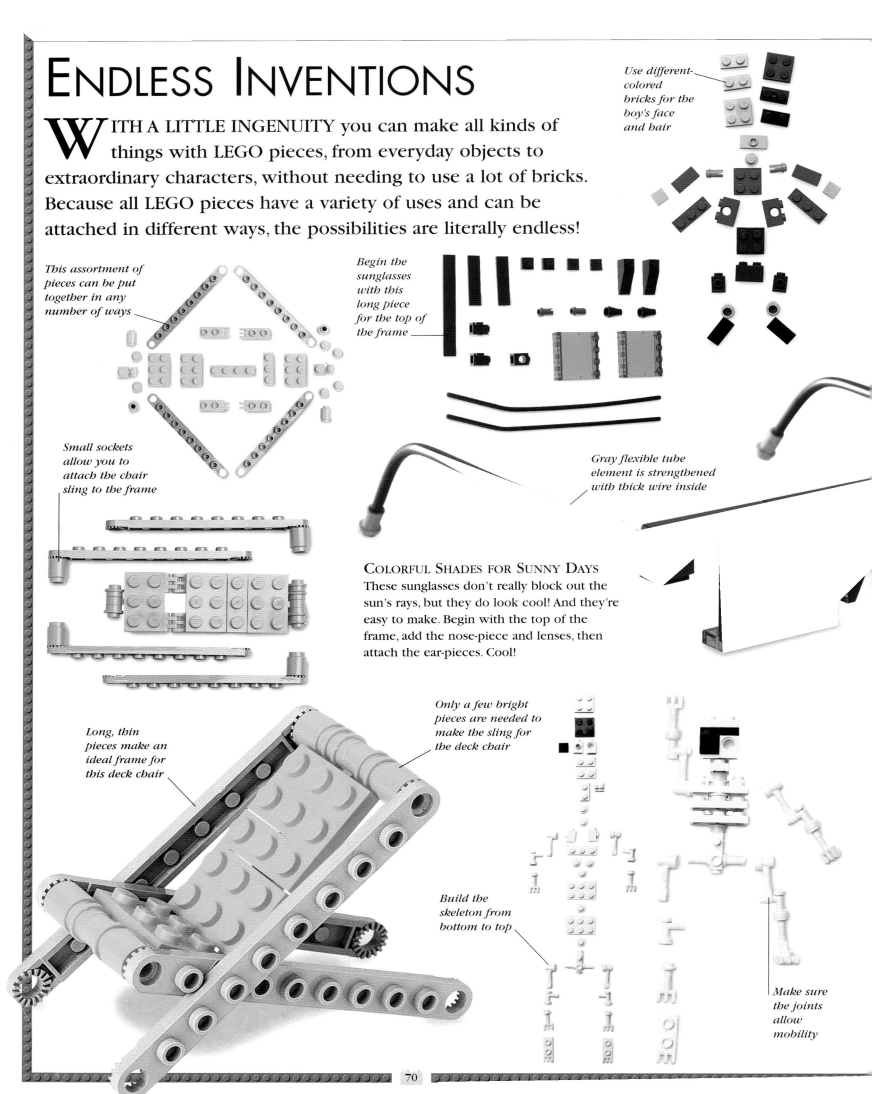

Use different-colored bricks for the boy's face and hair

This assortment of pieces can be put together in any number of ways

Begin the sunglasses with this long piece for the top of the frame

Small sockets allow you to attach the chair sling to the frame

Gray flexible tube element is strengthened with thick wire inside

COLORFUL SHADES FOR SUNNY DAYS
These sunglasses don't really block out the sun's rays, but they do look cool! And they're easy to make. Begin with the top of the frame, add the nose-piece and lenses, then attach the ear-pieces. Cool!

Long, thin pieces make an ideal frame for this deck chair

Only a few bright pieces are needed to make the sling for the deck chair

Build the skeleton from bottom to top

Make sure the joints allow mobility

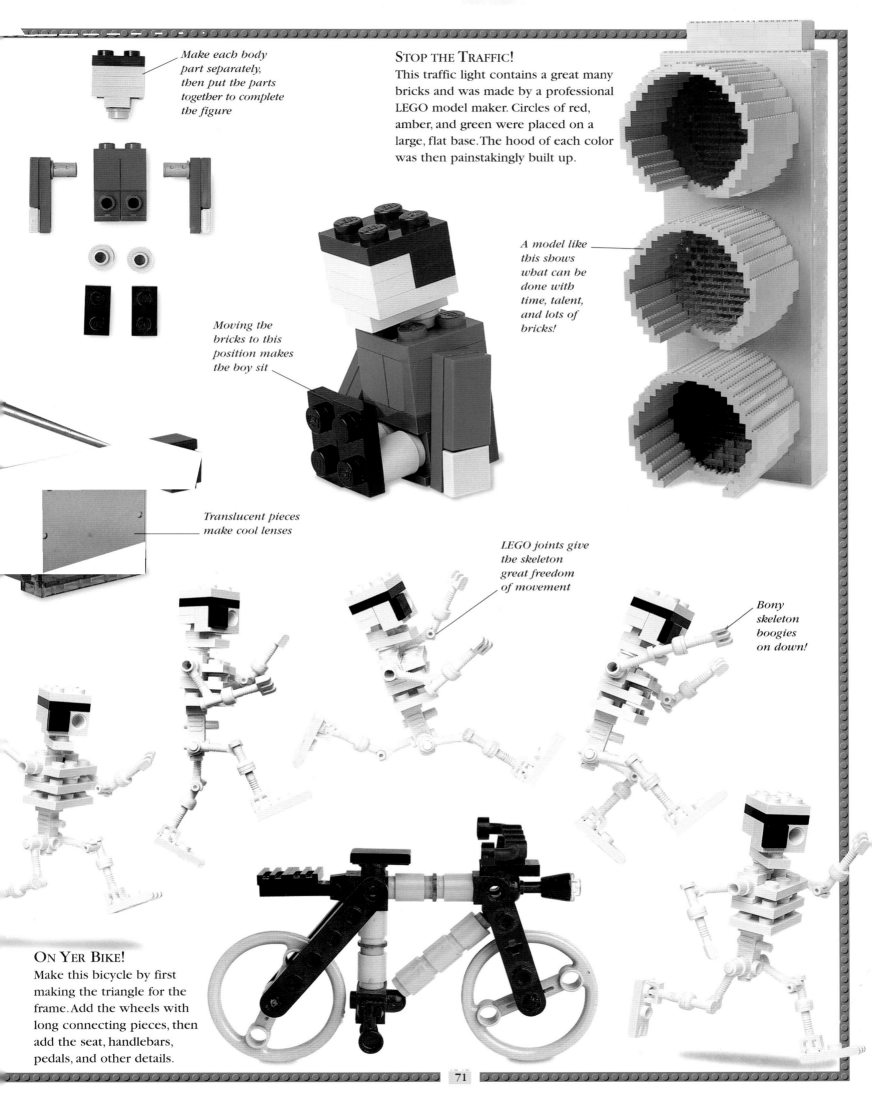

Make each body part separately, then put the parts together to complete the figure

STOP THE TRAFFIC!

This traffic light contains a great many bricks and was made by a professional LEGO model maker. Circles of red, amber, and green were placed on a large, flat base. The hood of each color was then painstakingly built up.

A model like this shows what can be done with time, talent, and lots of bricks!

Moving the bricks to this position makes the boy sit

Translucent pieces make cool lenses

LEGO joints give the skeleton great freedom of movement

Bony skeleton boogies on down!

ON YER BIKE!

Make this bicycle by first making the triangle for the frame. Add the wheels with long connecting pieces, then add the seat, handlebars, pedals, and other details.

OLÉ! OLÉ!

Luckily, this toreador is not in any danger, and neither is the bull! The brilliantly conceived piece was made in 1992 by 14-year-old Alejandro Lora Dias from Chile. It won him a World Cup first prize in his age group.

The bright red costume is decorated with "gold" buttons and trim

Flat red bricks are attached together to make the cape

MIND OVER MATTER

This young participant in the LEGO World Cup chooses his bricks carefully as he builds his model for the judges.

YOUNG ARCHITECT

Andreas, from Austria, was a finalist in the World Cup 3–5 age group in 1992. He built a little LEGO village.

Alejandro worked particularly hard to get the toreador's pose exactly right

Made with roof bricks, this bull looks ready to charge!

LEGO CHAMPIONS

THE LEGO GROUP sponsors many competitions for both children and adults. The biggest is the LEGO World Cup, for which children create award-winning models. Hundreds of thousands of children take part in preliminary rounds, which are held in 23 countries. The finalists travel to Billund to build new models for the judges. Another popular, long-running competition is the tallest tower contest. Each year new attempts are made around the world and new records are set.

TALLEST TOWER
Competitions are frequently held to build the tallest tower from LEGO bricks. In August 1998 the world record was set at 82 ft (24.91 m) for a tower built by some 6,000 fans in Talinn, Estonia. Sections are built at ground level, then taken up in a crane and put in place on the tower. If the tower is to remain on exhibit, it is reinforced with metal bars to prevent accidents.

PINOCCHIO
This ingenious version of the famous children's character was built by nine-year-old Neil Nastanski from the USA and won the Intermediate Group in 1992.

The transportation center includes an elevated train, ground-level train, and airport

Details include Pinocchio's extra-long LEGO brick nose

TRANSPORTATION CENTER
Five-year-old Thomas Michon from the USA built this transport hub of the future, winning 1992's youngest group.

DESIGN DECISIONS
With 764 pieces plus a motor and a battery box, Tina, from Switzerland, has her work cut out for her in the LEGO World Cup! What would you make?

THE LEGOLAND PARKS

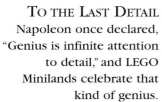

Donkey from LEGOREDO at LEGOLAND, Billund

I N THE 1960S, many people used to travel great distances to visit the LEGO factories in Billund, Denmark – over 20,000 every year. They were particularly interested in the LEGO models on display, many created by senior LEGO designer Dagny Holm. Godtfred Kirk Christiansen noticed this and wondered if it might be possible to move the models outdoors. He originally thought of a small garden tended by a couple of retired people, and he ended up with LEGOLAND Billund!

TO THE LAST DETAIL

Napoleon once declared, "Genius is infinite attention to detail," and LEGO Minilands celebrate that kind of genius.

Concept sketch for helicopter ride, Carlsbad

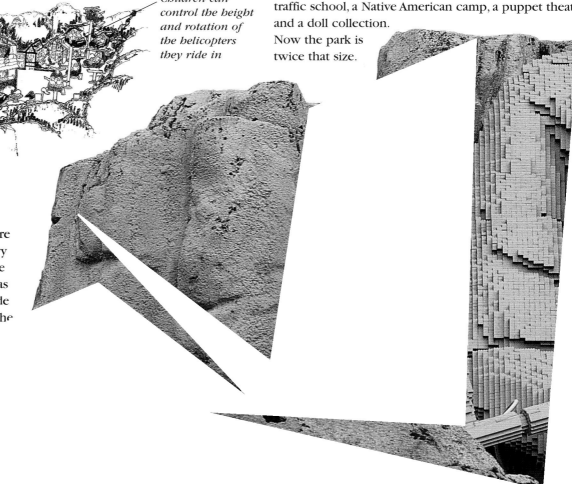

Children can control the height and rotation of the helicopters they ride in

EARLY DAYS

When LEGOLAND Billund opened on June 7, 1968, it covered an area of 41,557 square yards (38,000 sq m), and Miniland was accompanied by a LEGO train ride, a traffic school, a Native American camp, a puppet theate and a doll collection. Now the park is twice that size.

CORE ATTRACTIONS

Besides Miniland, there are certain core attractions that are a vital part of every LEGOLAND park. These are mainly the interactive rides in which the child has control. Classic core attractions include the driving school for junior drivers, the boat driving school, and the helicopter ride.

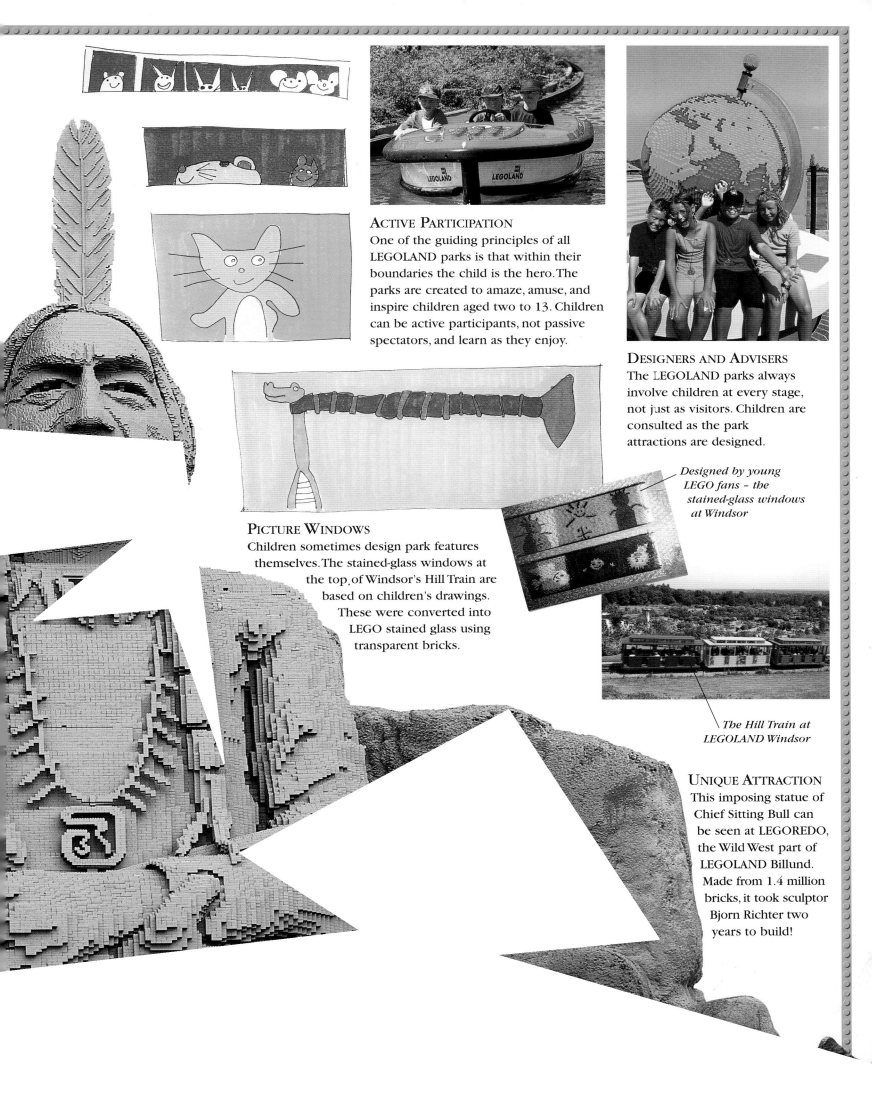

ACTIVE PARTICIPATION

One of the guiding principles of all LEGOLAND parks is that within their boundaries the child is the hero. The parks are created to amaze, amuse, and inspire children aged two to 13. Children can be active participants, not passive spectators, and learn as they enjoy.

DESIGNERS AND ADVISERS

The LEGOLAND parks always involve children at every stage, not just as visitors. Children are consulted as the park attractions are designed.

Designed by young LEGO fans – the stained-glass windows at Windsor

PICTURE WINDOWS

Children sometimes design park features themselves. The stained-glass windows at the top of Windsor's Hill Train are based on children's drawings. These were converted into LEGO stained glass using transparent bricks.

The Hill Train at LEGOLAND Windsor

UNIQUE ATTRACTION

This imposing statue of Chief Sitting Bull can be seen at LEGOREDO, the Wild West part of LEGOLAND Billund. Made from 1.4 million bricks, it took sculptor Bjorn Richter two years to build!

PLANNING THE PARKS

WHEN IT OPENED in 1968, LEGOLAND Billund appeared to break two of the basic rules for theme parks. It was sited a long way from large population centers, and it did not have a hot, sunny climate. However, from the very start it proved a paradise for families, and it now attracts more than a million people every year. As the LEGO Group saw LEGOLAND Billund becoming ever more successful, its leaders began to wonder if other parks could be set up in other parts of the world. Would LEGOLAND theme parks be successful in other countries? It was time to plan.

One of the concept drawings for Carlsbad

THE BLUE SKY

First of all, the concept team designed a "blue sky" park, a perfect LEGOLAND park, without regard to the limitations of an actual site. Doing this enabled them to decide the vital attractions of a LEGOLAND park. Then they could start working on the concepts for individual parks.

THE CONCEPT

Time is spent deciding where to put the park and working out a business plan. After this, a massive "Silver Book" (so called because it was first printed on silver paper) is prepared in which the total concept for the park is described.

WHERE IN THE WORLD?

The next question LEGOLAND park planners had to ask themselves was where to put the park. The world is a big place. Is it more important to site the park in a sunny part of the world or in a country with a proven enthusiasm for LEGO products? By siting the second park in rainy England, the LEGOLAND park planners opted for the latter. The success of Windsor showed that enthusiasm for LEGO constructions is more important than hours of sunshine. By siting the third park at Carlsbad, near San Diego in southern California, they managed to have the best of both worlds.

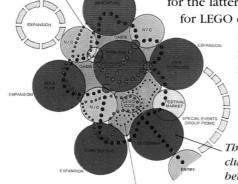

There is a nature cluster area between each of the active clusters

CONCEPT CLUSTERS

This is the initial concept map of the Carlsbad park, from the Silver Book. It shows the six main areas of activity, known as clusters: Miniland, DUPLO Village, Fun Town, Castle Hill, the Imagination Center, and the Beginning.

TELLING THE STORY

The concept design team members express the atmosphere that they wish each part of the park to possess by creating a story about it. The stories are written from the point of view of a child exploring the park.

THIS WAY, HURRY!

THE JOURNEY BEGINS
The guests enter the ride beneath an old rope bridge. Polly sitting nearby offers encouragement "this way!"

THE MAP! THE MAP!

THE WRECKED PIRATE SHIP (BOARDING POINT)
An Old Sea Captain is tied to the mast of his sunken ship. In his hand is the torn remnant of a treasure map. Spinosa, the monkey has come to his rescue whilst his parrot, Polly, squawks "The Map! The Map!"

THE OLD ELEVATOR
The flume abruptly ends and the vessels are lifted towards the sacred tree. Near the top the tall Pirate has one last chance to prevent the guests reaching the treasure. Axe in hand, he tries to cut the rope system hauling the boats. However, Spinosa comes to the rescue again.

THE PIRATES SURPRISED
Rounding a rock we come upon the pirates. A short fat pirate is taking from a rock but has only managed to catch an old boot. His tall friend has been bathing. Polly is trying to pull away his trousers which he is using to hide his embarrassment. The young girl visitor, whilst trying to avoid seeing the bathing pirate, doesn't notice Spinosa stealing the stolen treasure map.

Mood boards are created for each major area of the park to help the park designers and model builders

301 - Miniland   New York City Mood Board - 301.3

PICTURE THE MOOD

Another way of indicating the atmosphere desired for different parts of the park is to create a photo-collage called a "mood board", such as this one for the New York area of Miniland.

LOOK IN OR LOOK OUT?

The Windsor park is built to encourage visitors to enjoy the views. Billund and Carlsbad are very flat, so the parks are designed with a central focus. At Carlsbad, a lagoon was created at the heart of the park, with Miniland built on terraces around it.

Before beginning construction at Windsor, the LEGO Group had to demolish the buildings of the safari park that had occupied the site

PROBLEMS OR OPPORTUNITIES?

Each park has its own peculiarities. The Windsor site originally contained over 400 ancient, protected trees. The LEGO Group decided from the outset not only to keep every tree but to increase their number. Now, Windsor's "Wild Woods" area really makes the most of their imposing beauty.

DESIGNING IN DETAIL

ONCE THE BASIC CONCEPT for the park has been laid out in the Silver Book, a Green Book is created for each section. These Green Books are used to translate rough ideas into plans. Sketches are made into precise drawings, and each part of the park is mapped out. When the Green Books are complete, the consultants are able to make detailed construction drawings and the model builders can begin building the prototypes.

THE MASTER PLAN
At the Green Book stage, the original concept plan for the park (above) is developed into the final master plan. This works out the general area and shape of each part of the park.

Each Green Book is a substantial document, roughly 100 pages long

Document B.2.6
October 1996
Green Book

ent Definition

Document B.2.5
October 1996
Green Book

Innerpark - IMAGINATION CENTER
Concept Definition

LEGOLAND

A model of one of the mini areas in Miniland to help the model builders design individual components

Color and texture have been added to this later 3-D model to make it more realistic

NEW ORLEANS

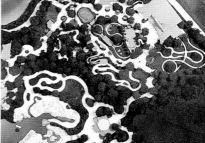

THE GREEN BOOKS
The Miniland and Imagination Center Green Books (left) are typical. They contain plans, elevations, and sections of each major component of the park, including strategies on architectural landscaping, food, and retail.

PLANNING IN 3D
Once the master plan has been made, a 3-D model of it is created to help the LEGOLAND team to visualize what the park will be like.

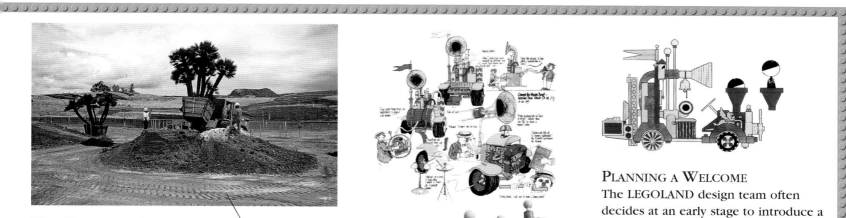

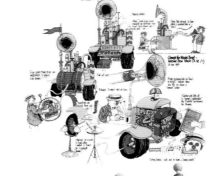

NOT BUILT IN A DAY

Planning and building parks can take more than four years. It takes 12–18 months to decide on the site and work out the product strategy and business plan. Making the models can take up to three years. Finally, the finished park requires 3–4 months of testing.

Building works at Carlsbad

PLANNING A WELCOME

The LEGOLAND design team often decides at an early stage to introduce a new feature, for example, the Welcome Wagon at Windsor. This began life as a drawing (above left) in the Windsor Silver Book. When the Green Books were created, a detailed drawing was done (above), from which the final vehicle was made.

The Welcome Wagon serves as a drivable, multipurpose "stage" for the Welcome Show at Windsor

TESTING TOTEM

Totem poles like this one were sent to the Carlsbad site to see if the strong California sun would fade the colors of the LEGO bricks faster than the Danish and English sunshine.

NIGHT LIGHTS

Each new park has special attractions, such as the maze on the Ridge at Carlsbad. Other attractions at Carlsbad include the animated night lighting in Miniland, for which the warm Californian evenings are perfect.

IN THE FUTURE

Each aspect of an attraction is sketched in detail to show exactly what kind of experience a visitor can expect.

LEGOLAND BILLUND

WHEN LEGOLAND BILLUND was opened in 1968, no one imagined just how popular it would prove to be. In 1996 the park welcomed its 25 millionth visitor and it now greets close to 1.5 million LEGO lovers every year. Most young Danes pay at least one visit to LEGOLAND Billund in their lives – as do a great many children and their parents from all over the world.

Early LEGO sculptures were less sophisticated than today's models because model makers had only basic bricks to work with

Over four to five years, the colors of the bricks fade

ON SAFARI
Children can steer small, zebra-striped jeeps on safari, meeting life-size lions, crocodiles, gorillas, rhinos, and other animals.

MAP OF HAPPINESS
This 1974 map showed many a child the path to attractions as different as Miniland and Titania's Palace. The palace is one of the most magnificent doll's houses in the world.

HOME BAKING
In the Indian Camp at LEGOREDO Town in the Wild West part of the park – pictured here in 1968, the year it opened – children bake their own twist bread under the watchful eye of Chief Playing Eagle.

BUSY ROADS
From its early days, one of the most popular attractions at Billund has been the Traffic School for young drivers. In the early days, cyclists were also allowed.

MINIATURE GARDENS
One of the features of Billund is its plants, which are scaled down to match the buildings. Two gardeners and 15 assistant gardeners are busy all year keeping it in order. They plant 60,000 flowers and 50,000 bulbs every year.

Copenhagen's Royal Rosenborg Castle

TOWERING ACHIEVEMENT
Spectacular animals, such as this elephant, are a speciality of the model builders, and they are hugely popular attractions.

The brighter colors and more realistic shape of these giraffes show that they are newer than the ones on the opposite page

BORN TO ROAM
These giraffes look so lifelike that you feel they should be striding across the park, loping from the Traffic School to the exciting new Mindstorms center.

KEEN SPECTATOR
If only this vulture could fly, it would follow the children to the five big thematic areas of the park: Miniland, LEGOREDO Town, Pirateland, Castleland, and DUPLO Land.

Children can't wait to put their heads in this lion's mouth!

FOREVER YOUNG
DUPLO Land is a play area in the park that caters especially to younger LEGO fans.

This cheerful character expresses the atmosphere of the park

PARK SYMBOL
The Billund symbol is similar to the child-size models of LEGO people, named LEGO Friends, that dot the park.

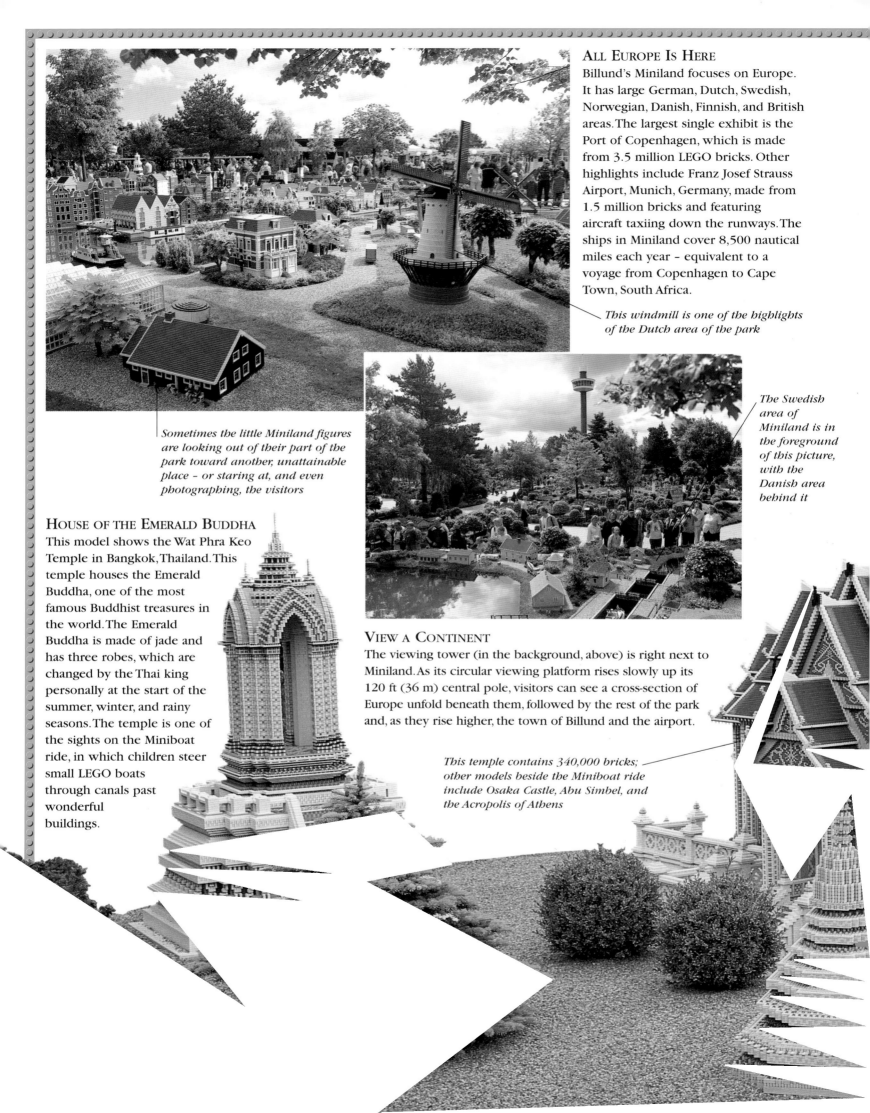

ALL EUROPE IS HERE

Billund's Miniland focuses on Europe. It has large German, Dutch, Swedish, Norwegian, Danish, Finnish, and British areas. The largest single exhibit is the Port of Copenhagen, which is made from 3.5 million LEGO bricks. Other highlights include Franz Josef Strauss Airport, Munich, Germany, made from 1.5 million bricks and featuring aircraft taxiing down the runways. The ships in Miniland cover 8,500 nautical miles each year – equivalent to a voyage from Copenhagen to Cape Town, South Africa.

This windmill is one of the highlights of the Dutch area of the park

Sometimes the little Miniland figures are looking out of their part of the park toward another, unattainable place – or staring at, and even photographing, the visitors

The Swedish area of Miniland is in the foreground of this picture, with the Danish area behind it

HOUSE OF THE EMERALD BUDDHA

This model shows the Wat Phra Keo Temple in Bangkok, Thailand. This temple houses the Emerald Buddha, one of the most famous Buddhist treasures in the world. The Emerald Buddha is made of jade and has three robes, which are changed by the Thai king personally at the start of the summer, winter, and rainy seasons. The temple is one of the sights on the Miniboat ride, in which children steer small LEGO boats through canals past wonderful buildings.

VIEW A CONTINENT

The viewing tower (in the background, above) is right next to Miniland. As its circular viewing platform rises slowly up its 120 ft (36 m) central pole, visitors can see a cross-section of Europe unfold beneath them, followed by the rest of the park and, as they rise higher, the town of Billund and the airport.

This temple contains 340,000 bricks; other models beside the Miniboat ride include Osaka Castle, Abu Simbel, and the Acropolis of Athens

A LEGO WORLD

THE VERY FIRST LEGO WORLD, named Miniland, was created at Billund in the 1960s, and it has been growing ever since. Miniland was the heart of the park then and it still is. At first, nearly all the buildings were Danish. Now it features buildings from all over Europe, with special examples from Asia and the Americas. It has taken many millions of bricks to build all the models that grace Miniland, and LEGOLAND Billund unveils a major new development almost every year.

THE OLSEN GANG
The Danish harbor area of Miniland has a special place for the three members of the Olsen gang, the central characters of a long-running series of Danish movies. Their theme tune plays in the background, and one of the ships in the harbor is constantly sending their catch phrase in Morse code.

The real temple is next to the Grand Palace in Bangkok

These guardians protect the temple

LAND OF MAGIC

ENCHANTMENT IS A major part of the recipe at LEGOLAND Billund. Children's imaginations are sure to stirred by the fantastic imaginary lands that they can actually enter, which are peopled with wonderful LEGO brick models that they can actually touch. Two of the most thrilling parts of the park are Pirateland, much of which can be viewed during an exciting boat ride, and the newest area, Castleland, which brilliantly evokes a medieval world of mystery, magic, and knightly deeds.

This jester welcomes visitors to the castle

A jolly pirate looks over visitors as they lunch in Pirateland

PIRATELAND
A pirate is marooned on a wild lagoon; sharks swim past, and guards man the fort in the background. This is Pirateland.

The colors of these new models are much more vivid than those of the old models behind them

FRIENDLY ROGUES
The pirate ship has a crew of ferocious-looking rogues. A boat trip into Captain Roger's secret cave takes guests past 15 different pirate scenes.

The black cat is so lifelike that it seems about to jump off the witch's back

CASTLELAND

The great castle was the big new attraction of 1997, and it was a huge hit. The LEGO scenes inside it recreate a magical medieval world, with dragons, knights in shining armor, lords, ladies, and comic servants. There is magic, humor, and drama.

A witch stares down into the wishing well

Shields like this one are affixed to the castle walls

MAGICAL RIDE

A dragon rollercoaster slides slowly past amazing medieval LEGO scenes, then speeds up for a dramatic twisting, turning climax.

At the top of the castle there is the Knight's Barbecue restaurant

The flags and towers add magic and romance to the skyline of the park

LEGOLAND WINDSOR

TWENTY-EIGHT YEARS after opening the first park in Billund, the LEGO Group opened its second park, in Windsor, England, in 1996. Built on the site of an old safari park, a great deal of work had to be done to get the park ready. Gardeners planted 60,000 trees and shrubs to complement the LEGO models. Completing the park – including producing all the models – took three years from start to finish.

This light-fingered fellow is about to drop into trouble

The model contains a large metal frame to provide extra support

DINOSAUR GREETINGS
A family of dinosaurs welcomes visitors when they arrive at LEGOLAND Windsor. Daddy Dinosaur cranes his neck over the park as he decides which attraction to visit first. Baby Dinosaur is about to hatch completely.

FAIR COP
Dotted around the park are life-size LEGO figures in lots of interesting poses – policemen, painters, and even the odd unsavory character!

IMPRESSIVE SITE

LEGOLAND Windsor is spread across rolling parkland in Berkshire. It was once part of the grounds of a stately home where the Kennedy family used to live when Joseph Kennedy was ambassador to the UK. From the highest part of the park, there are fantastic views over the town of Windsor and the Castle.

The town of Windsor and the Castle can be seen in the distance

Miniland lies at the heart of the park

Daddy Dinosaur is made from a quarter of a million LEGO bricks!

The German walled town of Rothenburg

Part of the Danish region of Jutland

DENMARK IN MINIATURE

The Danish area shows scenes from the Jutland region of the country, where the original LEGO bricks were created. In the real village of Skagen, the buildings are the same red and yellow shades as LEGO bricks.

GERMANY

The walled town of Rothenburg has been recreated in careful detail – even the beer festival is included!

Everyone's welcome at LEGOLAND Windsor – even junior dinosaurs!

HOLLAND

In this section of Miniland, Holland is represented both by the city of Amsterdam with its canals and gabled houses and by the Dutch countryside, which features lots of greenhouses and working windmills.

LITTLE BRITAIN

THE BRITISH AREA of Miniland contains some of the most famous and best-loved buildings in the country, as well as beautiful villages, famous castles, and natural landmarks such as Loch Ness. (You might even see the Loch Ness monster!) There's a model of ancient Stonehenge, a bustling harbor scene where trains shunt back and forth, unloading their cargo, and an air-sea rescue helicopter. The largest part of Little Britain is the historic capital city of London.

Beefeater from the Tower of London model

Pan pipe tunes and applause add realistic atmosphere

COVENT GARDEN

For hundreds of years Covent Garden market in central London was the main market for fruit, vegetables, and flowers. Now it is a very popular area for shopping, eating out, or going to the nearby theaters. Jugglers, comedians, and magicians entertain the crowds.

The famous chimes of Big Ben ring out across Miniland

BIG BEN

Most people believe the clock tower at the Houses of Parliament is called Big Ben, but in fact, it's the name of the bell inside.

The towers were not on Wren's plan; they were added in 1707

The cathedral is 360 ft (110 m) high; the model is 9 ft 3 in (2.85 m) tall

TOWER BRIDGE

There are 114,000 LEGO bricks used in the Tower Bridge model – enough to span the real River Thames 14 times if they were laid end to end. The drawbridge is raised when a tall ship needs to pass underneath.

The real St Paul's was designed by Sir Christopher Wren and started in 1675, after the old cathedral was destroyed in the Great Fire of 1666.

A loudspeaker concealed inside this part of the model broadcasts the cathedral bell accurately ringing the hour and quarter hour

St Paul's Cathedral
The St Paul's model used 380,000 bricks! If you stacked as many bricks, one on top of the other, the tower would be 2 miles (3.6 km) higher than the real cathedral.

ENDLESS ENTERTAINMENT

THE FUN NEVER STOPS at LEGOLAND Windsor! After the amazing Miniland models, why not get a licence at the LEGOLAND Driving School? One of the most popular attractions of every LEGOLAND park, the driving schools let children get behind the wheel of their own LEGO car and show their skill at negotiating major intersections, traffic lights, and of course, avoiding other cars!

OLD-FASHIONED STORIES
Famous Danish author Hans Christian Andersen has charmed children for generations with stories such as "The Ugly Duckling" and "The Emperor's New Clothes."

A NEW PERSPECTIVE
Capturing the moment on LEGO canvas, this artist is a resident of My Town.

READY FOR LIFTOFF!
It's hard work to winch yourself to the top of Space Tower. But then you can rappel all the way down!

These visitors have a bird's-eye view of LEGOLAND!

A LEGO road worker climbs out from the manhole for a cup of tea

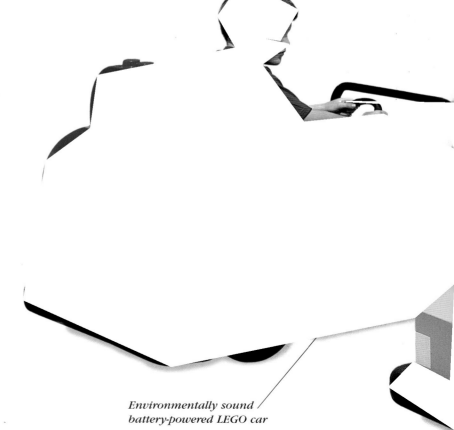

JOBS PEOPLE DO
Wherever you go in LEGOLAND Windsor, you'll see people working – but look closer, and you'll notice that some of the people are really LEGO figures!

Environmentally sound battery-powered LEGO car

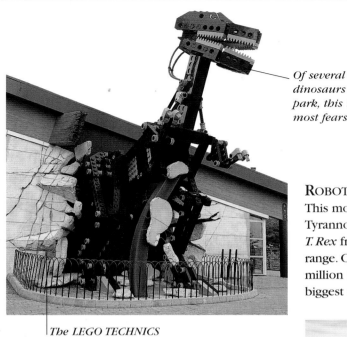

Of several dinosaurs in the park, this is the most fearsome!

ROBOT DINOSAUR

This moving model of the Tyrannosaurus is based on the *T. Rex* from the LEGO TECHNICS range. Composed of about a million bricks, the dinosaur is the biggest model in the park.

The LEGO TECHNICS Tyrannosaurus Rex looks as if it has just crashed through the wall!

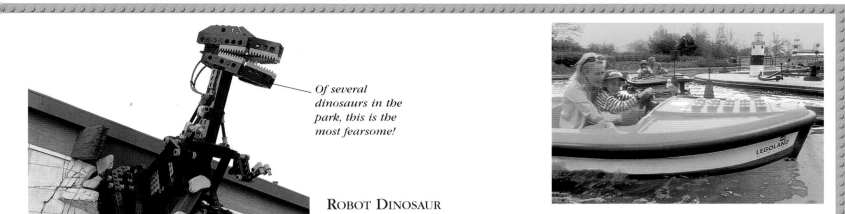

MAKING WAVES

Children can invite an adult along to zoom around at the LEGOLAND boating school. It's not as easy as it looks! Prospective sailors must look out for racing rapids, buoys, fishing boats, and other obstacles on the water.

Top speed in the cars is 6 mp/h (10 km/h)

RED LIGHT, GREEN LIGHT

Nearly half a million children are introduced to road safety every year in the driving school's 50 LEGO-style cars. Children not only learn to stop on red and go on green, but also to maneuver their cars on the roads, as they watch out for other traffic. When the young drivers pass their driving test, they receive a special LEGOLAND driver's licence.

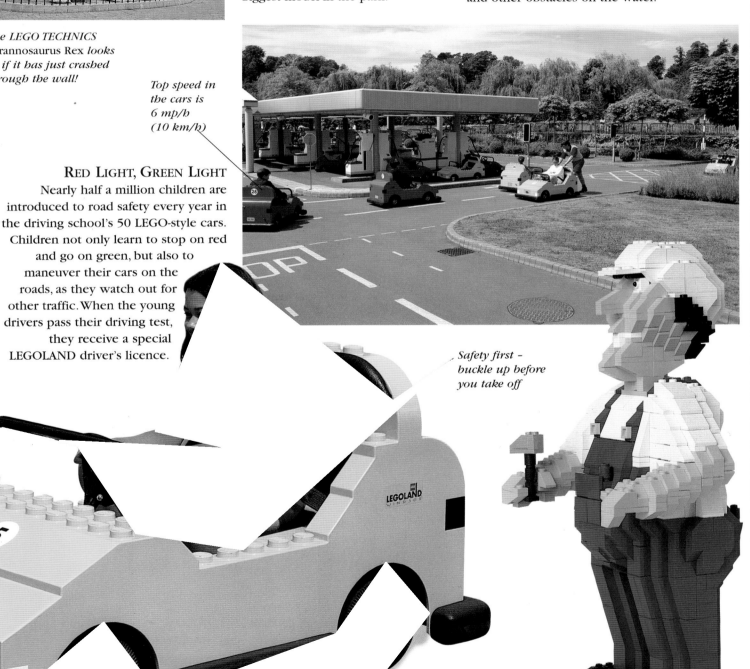

Safety first – buckle up before you take off

LEGOLAND California

I N MARCH 1999, the third LEGOLAND park opened in southern California. Here, the blue skies and sunshine combine with exciting attractions to create a child's paradise. Thirty million LEGO bricks have been used to make the more than 1,000 LEGO models that appear at the park! LEGOLAND California focuses on interactive entertainment, which blends fun and learning to create a unique experience.

GETTING READY FOR THE MAGIC
This is how the site looked when work began on LEGOLAND California. Building the LEGO models and the construction of the attractions took three years to finish.

Visitors love the attraction of a lake and riding in a boat

These ponds are quite shallow and safe for young children to walk alongside

FOCUS ON CHILDREN
LEGOLAND California offers fun and adventure for children and their families. The California park encompasses the best of the Billund and Windsor parks, like the LEGO driving school, as well as other brand-new attractions!

KID POWER TOWER
A massive crane swings into action as construction gets under way on the Kid Power Tower (right), which will provide excellent views across the park.

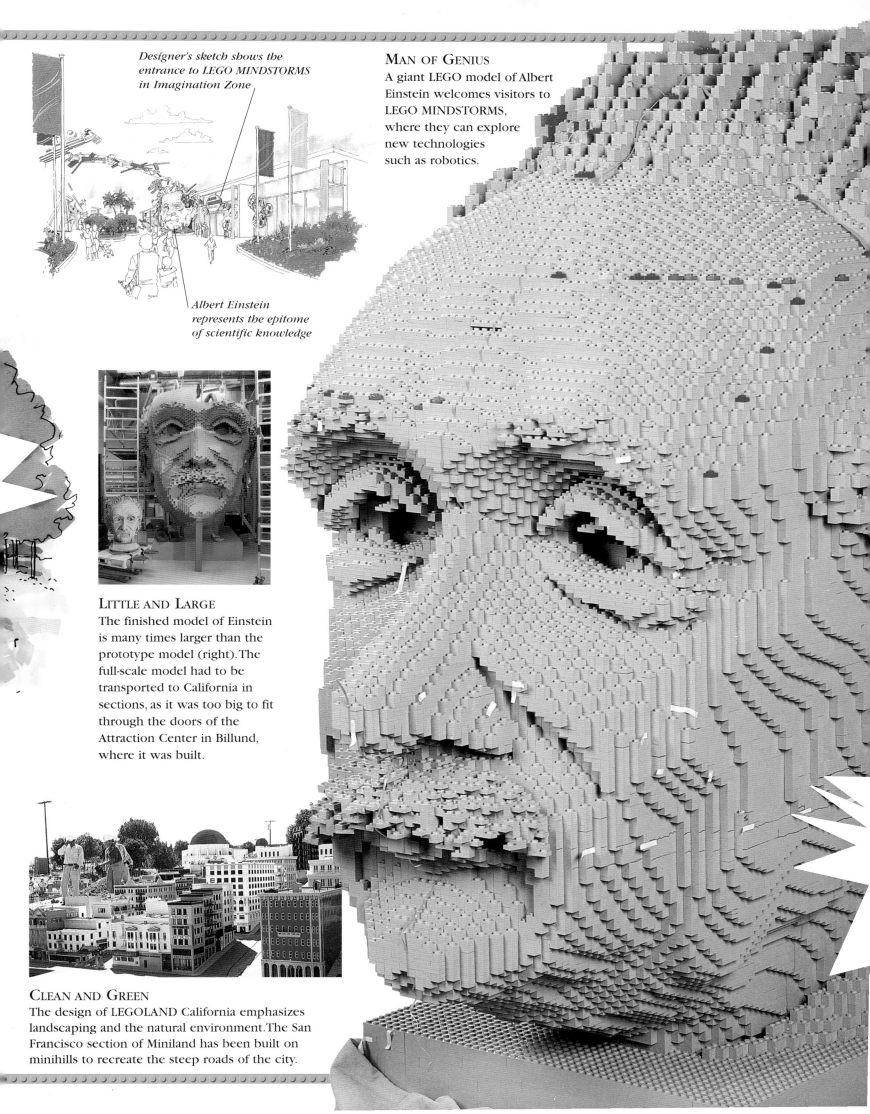

Designer's sketch shows the entrance to LEGO MINDSTORMS in Imagination Zone

Albert Einstein represents the epitome of scientific knowledge

MAN OF GENIUS

A giant LEGO model of Albert Einstein welcomes visitors to LEGO MINDSTORMS, where they can explore new technologies such as robotics.

LITTLE AND LARGE

The finished model of Einstein is many times larger than the prototype model (right). The full-scale model had to be transported to California in sections, as it was too big to fit through the doors of the Attraction Center in Billund, where it was built.

CLEAN AND GREEN

The design of LEGOLAND California emphasizes landscaping and the natural environment. The San Francisco section of Miniland has been built on minihills to recreate the steep roads of the city.

IMAGINATION ZONE

PLAY AS YOU LEARN is the motto at the Imagination Zone, one of the most exciting specially themed areas at LEGOLAND California. The Imagination Zone features a wacky environment designed to encourage children of all ages to imagine new and weird creations of their own. They can build and test their LEGO creations and even use new computerized bricks to make and control LEGO robots. There is a special activity area for the youngest LEGO fans. Of course, adults are welcome to join in, too!

MAGICAL MINI MACHINE
Mini figures fly this life-size model of the Time Machine. Model makers build miniature models to use as a prototype before proceeding to the larger LEGOLAND models.

SUBMERGING SUBMARINE
This LEGO submarine had to be carefully supported at the correct angle during construction. It is in place at LEGOLAND California, equipped with flashing lights, moving radar antennae, and a sliding periscope.

YELLOW SUBMARINE
To ensure the desired dramatic effect of a submerging sub, the model makers had to ensure that it would eventually be stable enough to stand unsupported. Here, the 20-ft (6-m) long submarine is transported on a dolly to its position at the entrance of the LEGO Workshop.

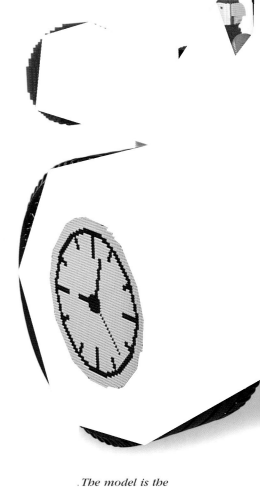

The heart of this huge dinosaur flashes, and smoke billows from his mouth

THIS IS WHERE THE FUN BEGINS
A 23-ft (7-m) high grinning LEGO TECHNIC *Tyrannosaurus rex* hovers over the workshops, daring young visitors to enter and play.

The model is the size of a real car

The Time Machine is suspended on a girder so that it seems to fly

Extra-large LEGO bricks "float" above Imagination Street

Life-size LEGO TECHNIC giraffes tower over the visitors

Climbing plants have been trained to grow over LEGO models of buffalo

ALL ABOUT STRUCTURE
The unusual façade of the Imagination Zone entices visitors in to play. It has an exciting range of activities for children of all ages, including LEGO building tables and an earthquake zone. Here, children can learn what makes tall structures stable and how to build them.

VRRRRROOOOOOOOM! HERE WE COME!
The Time Machine is a marvelous and unique creation. Its makers stretched their imaginations for this model, fusing elements from different kinds of vehicles, the body and wheels of a car, the rotor of a helicopter, and the launch blaster of a rocket!

BUILDING MINILAND

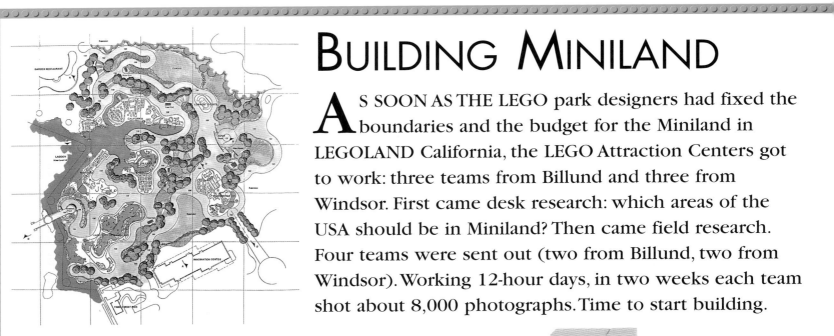

AS SOON AS THE LEGO park designers had fixed the boundaries and the budget for the Miniland in LEGOLAND California, the LEGO Attraction Centers got to work: three teams from Billund and three from Windsor. First came desk research: which areas of the USA should be in Miniland? Then came field research. Four teams were sent out (two from Billund, two from Windsor). Working 12-hour days, in two weeks each team shot about 8,000 photographs. Time to start building.

THE MINILAND PLAN

The overall plan for Miniland was created by the LEGOLAND design team, who continued to work with the Attraction Centers to fill out the plan. Detailed sketches such as those on the right were there to brief the builders.

Grand Central Station in the New York part of Miniland (see pages 48–49)

This posed a special design challenge: how to allow visitors to see inside the station

Information booth carries posters of upcoming events

EVERY DETAIL

For their research, the Attraction Center teams did not just photograph the major buildings, they even included smaller features such as this New York information booth, so that all the background details would be perfect.

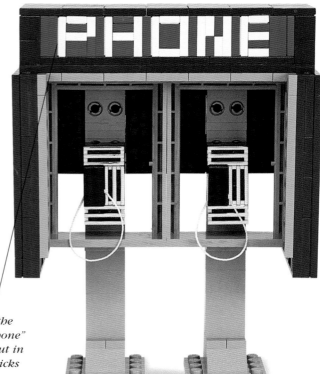

Details include the word "phone" picked out in LEGO bricks

DAILY LIFE

The smallest details of American streets were photographed and re-created for Miniland.

Wheelie bin

Parking meter

Fire hydrants

Trash can

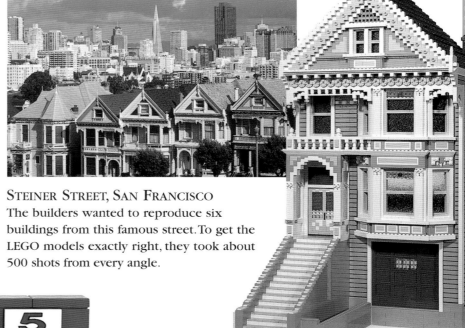

STEINER STREET, SAN FRANCISCO

The builders wanted to reproduce six buildings from this famous street. To get the LEGO models exactly right, they took about 500 shots from every angle.

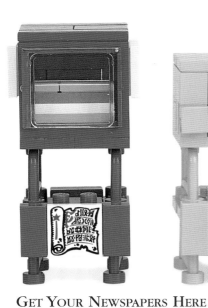

GET YOUR NEWSPAPERS HERE

One of the more unusual American customs is to buy a newspaper from a machine. If real Americans do it, so must the people of Miniland, and model makers have provided them with plenty of reading matter.

Newspaper dispensers come in various shapes, sizes, and colors

New York fire hydrants

RUBBISH TO RESEARCH

Any American passersby who saw strange visitors from Europe photographing their rubbish bins can now be enlightened: it was not madness but research!

All kinds of people are portrayed, including these nuns

Different clothes help give the nuns different characters

NEW ENGLAND

LOCATED IN THE NORTHEASTERN corner of the USA, New England is rich in history. The Pilgrims landed in Plymouth in 1620, and the American Revolution began in the city of Boston. Today, New England is an enchanting mix of quaint towns, wooded mountains, idyllic farms, and a scenic coast. The harbor in Miniland shows the impact of boats on work and leisure in New England.

HOLIDAY HAVEN
New England is famous for the spectacular autumn colors of the trees. The blaze of red, orange, and gold complements the blue sea.

HARBOR PLANS
Miniland designers sketched out this plan of the harbor area before the model makers started work. They particularly wanted to show the importance of New England's waterways.

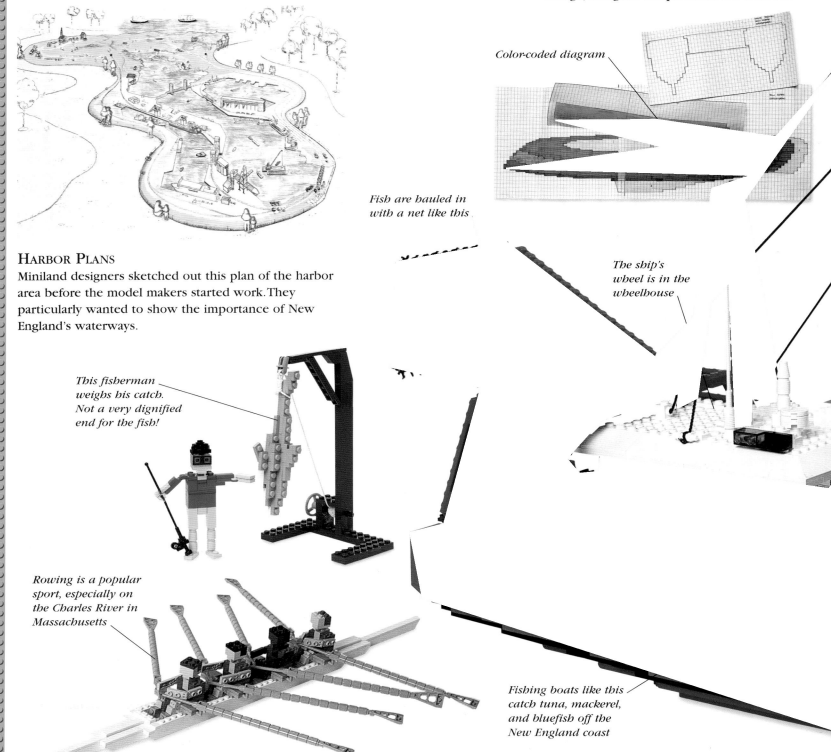

Color-coded diagram

Fish are hauled in with a net like this

The ship's wheel is in the wheelhouse

This fisherman weighs his catch. Not a very dignified end for the fish!

Rowing is a popular sport, especially on the Charles River in Massachusetts

Fishing boats like this catch tuna, mackerel, and bluefish off the New England coast

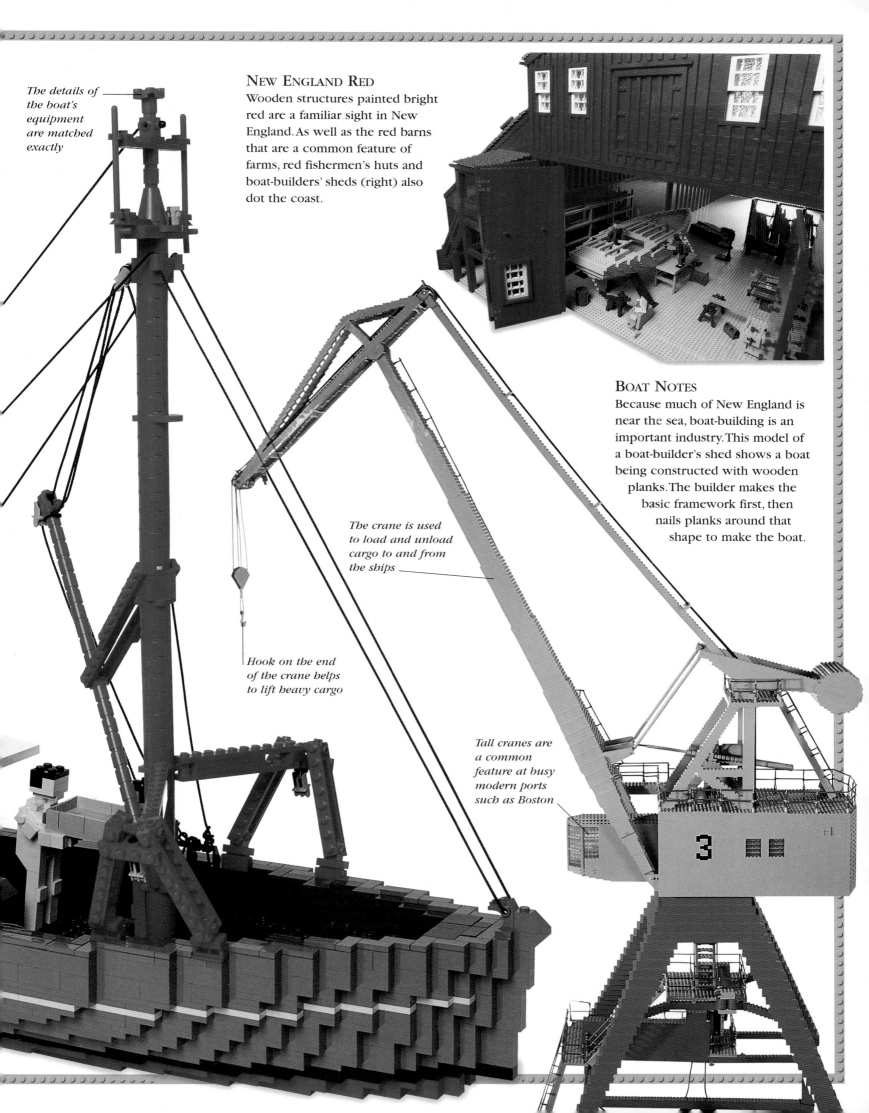

The details of the boat's equipment are matched exactly

NEW ENGLAND RED
Wooden structures painted bright red are a familiar sight in New England. As well as the red barns that are a common feature of farms, red fishermen's huts and boat-builders' sheds (right) also dot the coast.

BOAT NOTES
Because much of New England is near the sea, boat-building is an important industry. This model of a boat-builder's shed shows a boat being constructed with wooden planks. The builder makes the basic framework first, then nails planks around that shape to make the boat.

The crane is used to load and unload cargo to and from the ships

Hook on the end of the crane helps to lift heavy cargo

Tall cranes are a common feature at busy modern ports such as Boston

3

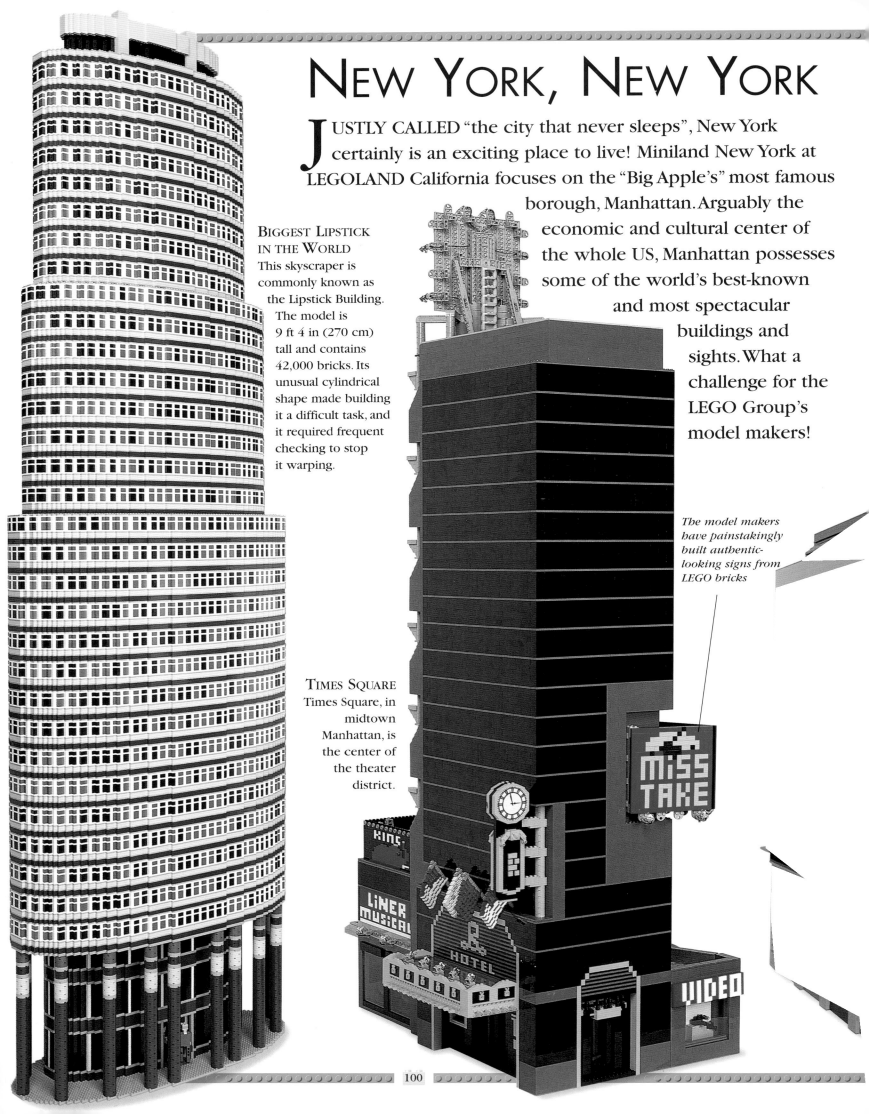

NEW YORK, NEW YORK

JUSTLY CALLED "the city that never sleeps", New York certainly is an exciting place to live! Miniland New York at LEGOLAND California focuses on the "Big Apple's" most famous borough, Manhattan. Arguably the economic and cultural center of the whole US, Manhattan possesses some of the world's best-known and most spectacular buildings and sights. What a challenge for the LEGO Group's model makers!

BIGGEST LIPSTICK IN THE WORLD
This skyscraper is commonly known as the Lipstick Building. The model is 9 ft 4 in (270 cm) tall and contains 42,000 bricks. Its unusual cylindrical shape made building it a difficult task, and it required frequent checking to stop it warping.

The model makers have painstakingly built authentic-looking signs from LEGO bricks

TIMES SQUARE
Times Square, in midtown Manhattan, is the center of the theater district.

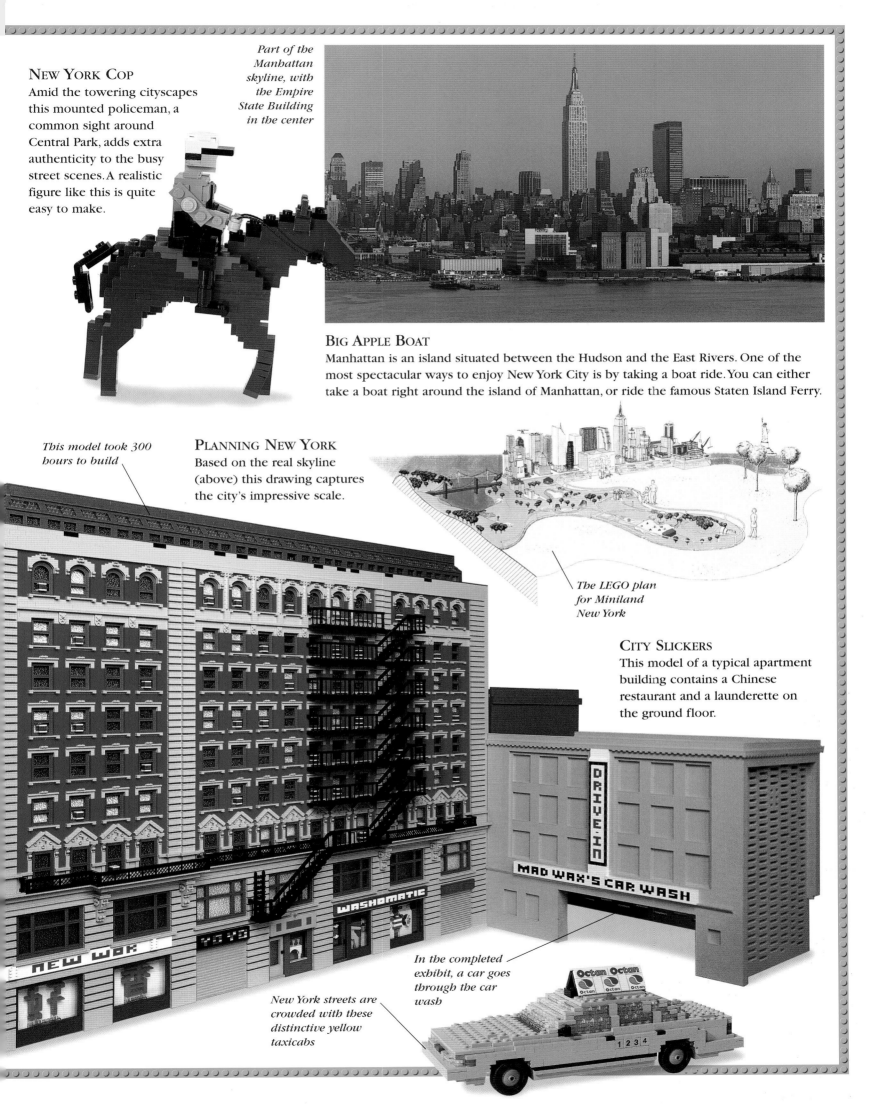

NEW YORK COP

Amid the towering cityscapes this mounted policeman, a common sight around Central Park, adds extra authenticity to the busy street scenes. A realistic figure like this is quite easy to make.

Part of the Manhattan skyline, with the Empire State Building in the center

BIG APPLE BOAT

Manhattan is an island situated between the Hudson and the East Rivers. One of the most spectacular ways to enjoy New York City is by taking a boat ride. You can either take a boat right around the island of Manhattan, or ride the famous Staten Island Ferry.

This model took 300 hours to build

PLANNING NEW YORK

Based on the real skyline (above) this drawing captures the city's impressive scale.

The LEGO plan for Miniland New York

CITY SLICKERS

This model of a typical apartment building contains a Chinese restaurant and a launderette on the ground floor.

WASHOMATIC

NEW WAX

DRIVE-IN

MAD WAX'S CAR WASH

In the completed exhibit, a car goes through the car wash

New York streets are crowded with these distinctive yellow taxicabs

Octan Octan

1 2 3 4

WASHINGTON, DC

ONE OF THE MAJOR Miniland attractions of LEGOLAND California is the Washington cluster. This exhibit features many of the most famous buildings in the US, including the seat of government power, the magnificent Capitol. This contains about 1,641,000 bricks, weighs 717 lb (326 kg), and took the model makers at Windsor more than 1,200 hours to build.

Miniland Washington includes the White House and the Washington Monument

A model maker is working on the central section of the Capitol

HIDDEN DETAILS
The Capitol model is made up of five main sections, plus the domed section. The dome contains a water tank, which feeds a nearby fountain.

The Old Post Office – this is now a shopping center

MUSICAL FUN
The model contains four speakers, one of which broadcasts brass-band music. But if they press buttons, children can make an out-of-tune trombone, bagpipes, or a jazzy saxophone join in.

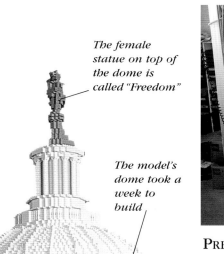

The female statue on top of the dome is called "Freedom"

The model's dome took a week to build

PRECISE MEASUREMENTS
A Windsor model maker checks the proportions of the model.

CLASSICAL ARCHITECTURE
Many hours of careful planning went into the construction of the elegant porticos of the Jefferson Memorial, which has 66 columns.

The Jefferson Memorial looks out onto the Tidal Basin

THE CAPITOL
This impressive building was completed in 1800. Since no building in Washington may be built to be taller than the top of the Capitol's dome, it dominates the Washington skyline. The LEGO model is 7ft 4in (2.2 m) high.

FASCINATING FACTS
The Memorial took 250 hours to build and contains about 39,800 bricks. As in real life, there is a statue of Thomas Jefferson, author of the Declaration of Independence, inside.

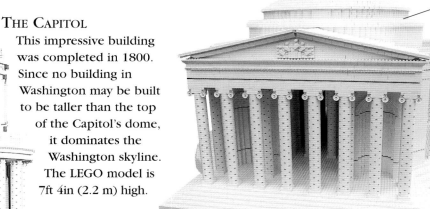

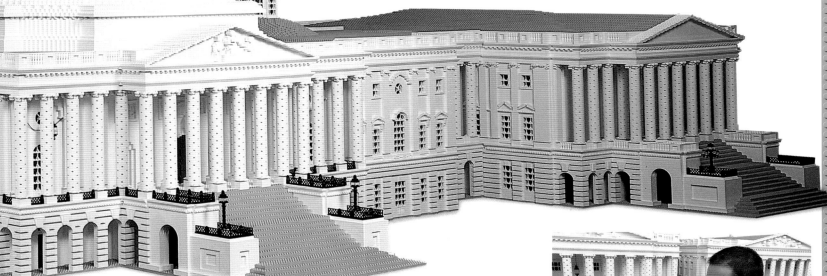

SPACIOUS MALL
The Mall is a large green area in the center of the city where many of the important government buildings and museums are located. The Capitol stands majestically at one end of the Mall.

EVERY LAST DETAIL
The finishing touches are added to the model of the Capitol.

MISSISSIPPI RIVER BOAT

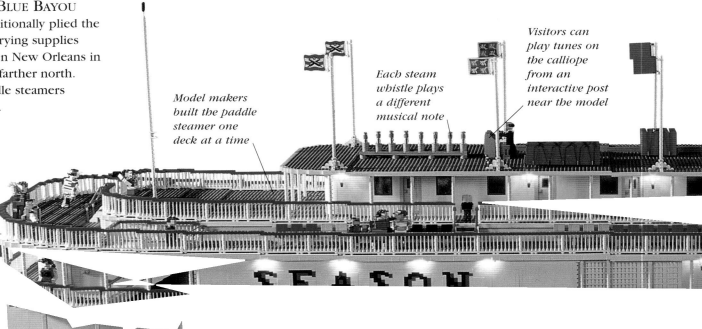

ONE OF THE HIGHLIGHTS of the New Orleans Miniland exhibit at LEGOLAND California is this fabulous paddle steamer, which sails along a miniature re-creation of the Mississippi River delta. Using special interactive animation, visitors can toot the ship's horn or play a Dixieland jazz tune on the miniature calliope on the top deck. But beware the alligators that rise to the surface of the water at the press of a button!

BOATING ON THE BLUE BAYOU
Paddle steamers traditionally plied the Mississippi River carrying supplies and produce between New Orleans in the south and stops farther north. These days, the paddle steamers mainly carry visitors.

As the paddlewheel turns, the blades dip into the water and push the boat along

Model makers built the paddle steamer one deck at a time

Each steam whistle plays a different musical note

Visitors can play tunes on the calliope from an interactive post near the model

Sixty small lights illuminate the inside of the model

The model weighs 308 lb (140 kg) and took 500 hours to build

ON THE DECK
Model makers create little scenarios for the Mini figures to bring large models to life. On the LEGO paddle steamer's deck are tourists, a family on a special outing, and an elderly couple celebrating their wedding anniversary.

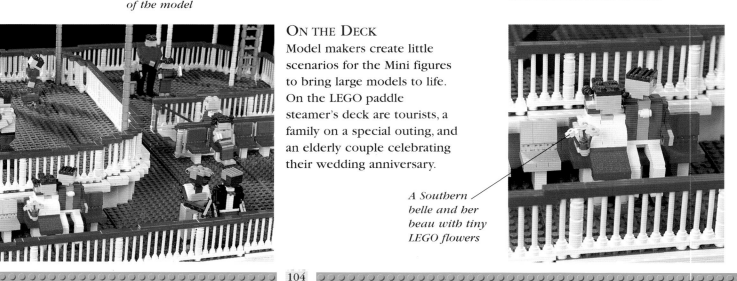

A Southern belle and her beau with tiny LEGO flowers

MISSISSIPPI CRUISING

There's nothing quite like feeling the sultry breeze coming off the Mississippi River during a paddle-steamer cruise. Near its delta, the mighty Mississippi fans out into shallow swamps known as bayous.

The model is 4 ft *(1 metre 40 cm) t*

Details include miniature viewfinders on the forward decks

The paddle steamer is more than 13 ft (4 metres) long

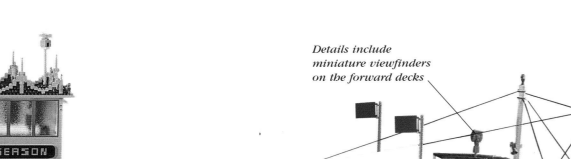

A hidden mechanism beneath the boat enables the paddle steamer to move in the water

Model makers ensure the boat will "float" in the LEGO bayou

The paddlewheel turns on its axle

LEGO CHARACTERS

Model makers give Mini figures distinctive characteristics through details such as the hats on these children.

MARDI GRAS

N EW ORLEANS is renowned all over the world for the Mardi Gras festival, one of the largest street carnivals in the world. At LEGO Miniland, the spirit and energy of Mardi Gras is recreated in all its exuberant glory. Model makers have even built special animated floats for the magnificent parade. LEGO brick spectators add to the fun with their colorful costumes.

Fabulous Mardi Gras headdresses

KING FOR A DAY

In New Orleans, months of hard work go into the designing and building of these huge ornate floats. At Miniland, the LEGO floats may be smaller, but model makers still require many weeks to plan and construct each one.

Every detail of the LEGO costumes was based on real Mardi Gras costumes

Quirky details such as this parasol add to the realism

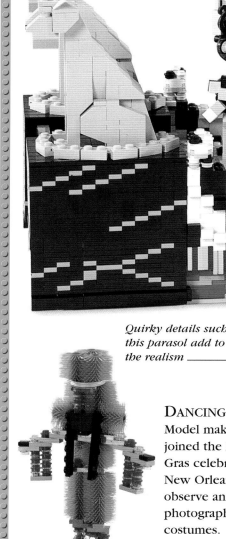

DANCING QUEEN

Model makers joined the Mardi Gras celebrations in New Orleans to observe and photograph many costumes.

Tiny beads simulate the traditional Mardi Gras necklaces that are thrown to the crowds

There are as many different ways of making a costume as there are LEGO bricks

Marchers carry the Mardi Gras Queen

The bull is a symbol of fertility

THE COLORFUL CITY
Every street in the old town fills to the brim with revelers – dancing, singing, or just watching it all go by.

This horn of plenty float celebrates the coming of spring

A small motor beneath each float enables it to move

FLOAT OF PLENTY
LEGO-brick floats parade past visitors in a riot of color. This one is covered with expertly crafted flowers and fruit.

QUICK MARCH!
Marchers begin practicing well before Mardi Gras. These LEGO Mini figures are positioned so that they are exactly in step with each other.

STAR GAZING

O NE OF THE MAJOR landmarks in LEGOLAND California is the impressive model of Griffith Observatory, which is built into the natural slope of a hill. Visitors to the park can look at the stars through an interactive telescope or view the splendor of Hollywood below, where they can spot a number of colorful classic and modern cars, reflecting the excitement and glamor of life in Los Angeles, the movie capital of the world.

OBSERVING THE OBSERVATORY
The model of the Griffith Observatory weighs 805 lb (366 kg) and contains around 36,000 LEGO bricks.

HILLTOP VIEW
The real Griffith Observatory is located in the 4,000-acre (1,620-hectare) Griffith Park. People visit the park to escape the crowds and view the city below.

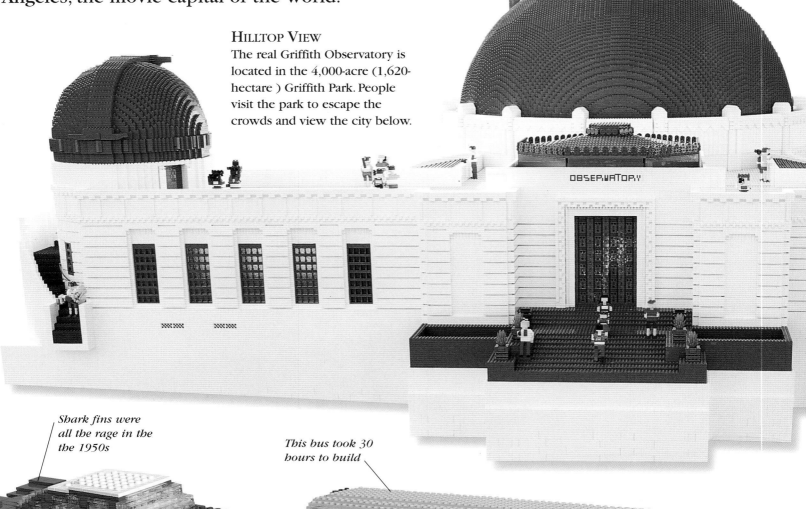

OBSERVATORY

Shark fins were all the rage in the the 1950s

This bus took 30 hours to build

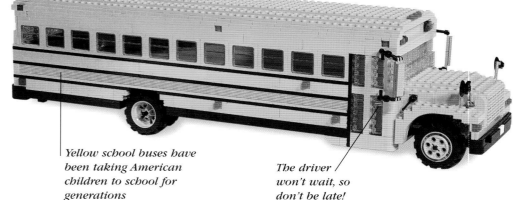

CAR CRAZY
Reflecting Americans' lasting love affair with the automobile, California Miniland contains some excellent models of classic cars. The fancy wheels on these pages each took an average of 20 hours to build and each one contains about 500 bricks.

Yellow school buses have been taking American children to school for generations

The driver won't wait, so don't be late!

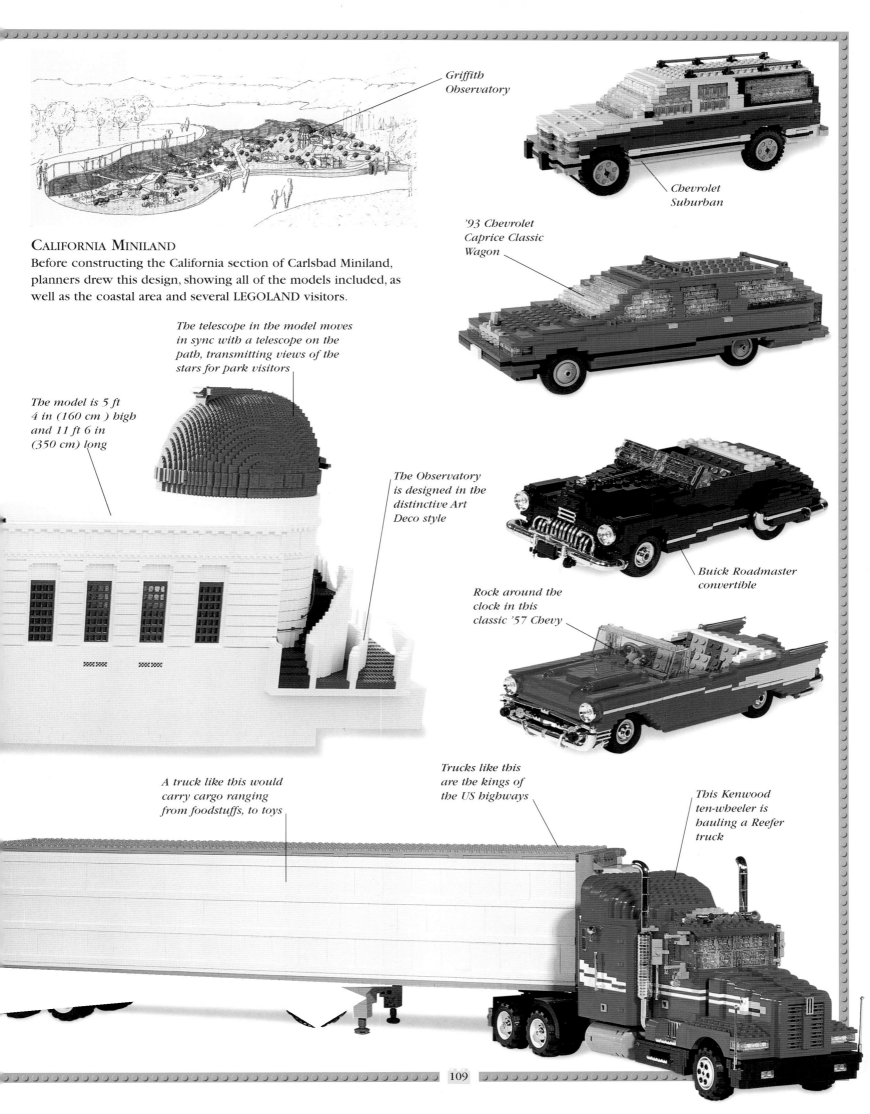

Griffith
Observatory

Chevrolet
Suburban

'93 Chevrolet
Caprice Classic
Wagon

CALIFORNIA MINILAND

Before constructing the California section of Carlsbad Miniland, planners drew this design, showing all of the models included, as well as the coastal area and several LEGOLAND visitors.

The telescope in the model moves in sync with a telescope on the path, transmitting views of the stars for park visitors

The model is 5 ft 4 in (160 cm) high and 11 ft 6 in (350 cm) long

The Observatory is designed in the distinctive Art Deco style

Buick Roadmaster convertible

Rock around the clock in this classic '57 Chevy

A truck like this would carry cargo ranging from foodstuffs, to toys

Trucks like this are the kings of the US highways

This Kenwood ten-wheeler is hauling a Reefer truck

GINGERBREAD HOUSE

San Francisco's famous Steiner Street is lined with picturesque clapboard houses. The LEGO models are just as colorful as the originals.

Decorative details on the gabled roof

The house is 2 ft 7 in (79 cm) high

BUILDING THE GOLDEN GATE

A special dark orange shade of brick was used to match the color of the real bridge. The model can be seen from both Miniland and the Family Boat Ride on the lagoon.

ACROSS THE BAY

The Golden Gate Bridge is San Francisco's best-known landmark. Opened in 1937, it spans the bay to connect San Francisco with Marin County.

The real bridge is 1.6 miles (2.7 km) long and carries 40 million vehicles a year

FISHERMAN'S FUN

Fishermen from Italy settled in the wharf area in the late 1800s. The area now features numerous restaurants that serve fish freshly caught in the bay. Tourists can also enjoy museums, shops, and amusements, or they can visit the sea lions that nap on the docks.

Sea Place

SALADS   CRABS   SEAFOOD   BREAD

SAN FRANCISCO

COLORFUL, LIVELY, and thriving, Miniland San Francisco at LEGOLAND California features the city's distinctive wooden houses, noisy, vibrant Chinatown, the bustle of Fisherman's Wharf, and the magnificent Golden Gate Bridge. LEGOLAND visitors are guaranteed plenty of fun looking at the models of parts of this beautiful city.

CHINATOWN
The city's thriving Chinese-American culture is accurately reflected in the Chinatown section, with its elaborate pagodas and colorful shops and restaurants.

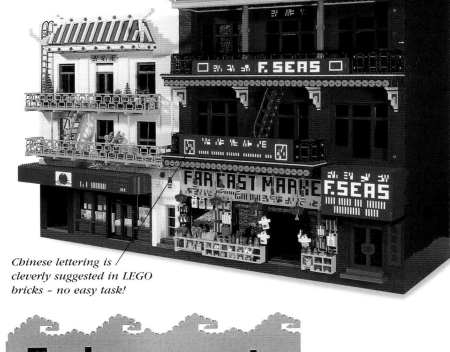

A Chinese pagoda sits atop the market

Chinese lettering is cleverly suggested in LEGO bricks – no easy task!

EASTERN PROMISE
Goods from the Far East are sold in the markets of Chinatown, home of the fortune cookie. An ambient soundtrack accompanies the model.

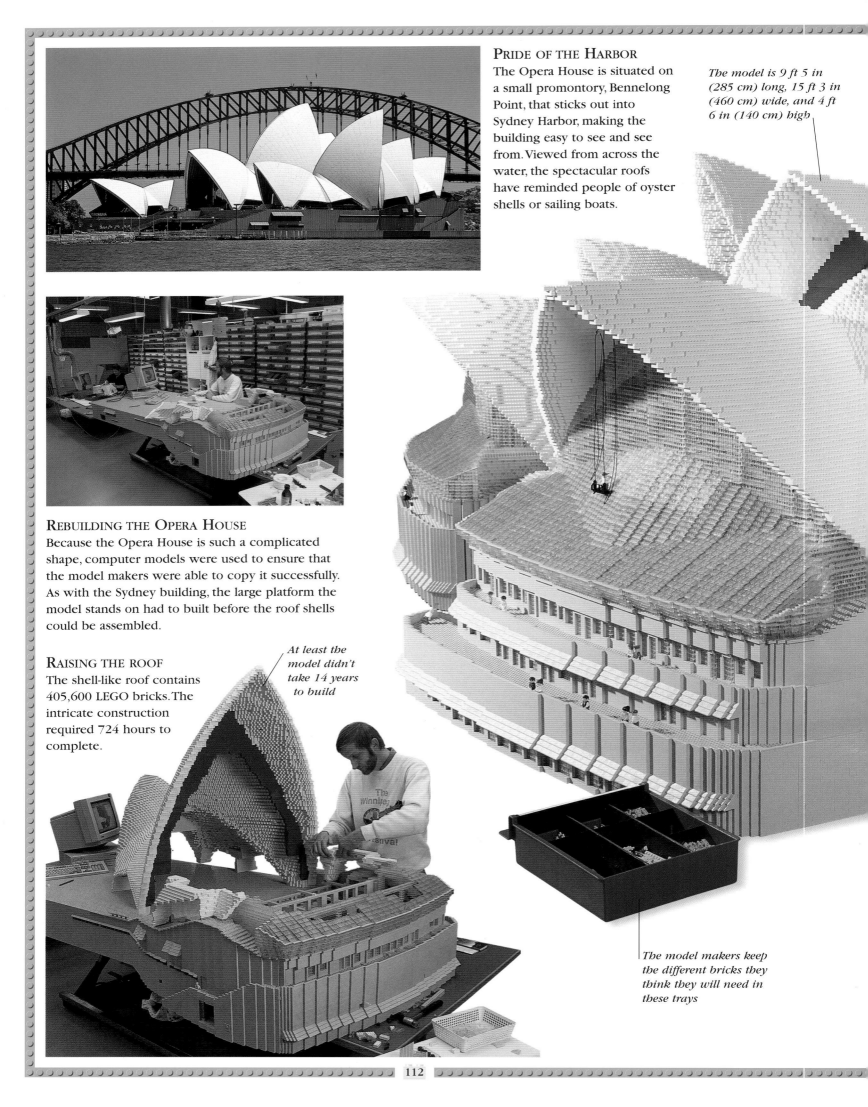

PRIDE OF THE HARBOR

The Opera House is situated on a small promontory, Bennelong Point, that sticks out into Sydney Harbor, making the building easy to see and see from. Viewed from across the water, the spectacular roofs have reminded people of oyster shells or sailing boats.

The model is 9 ft 5 in (285 cm) long, 15 ft 3 in (460 cm) wide, and 4 ft 6 in (140 cm) high

REBUILDING THE OPERA HOUSE

Because the Opera House is such a complicated shape, computer models were used to ensure that the model makers were able to copy it successfully. As with the Sydney building, the large platform the model stands on had to built before the roof shells could be assembled.

RAISING THE ROOF

The shell-like roof contains 405,600 LEGO bricks. The intricate construction required 724 hours to complete.

At least the model didn't take 14 years to build

The model makers keep the different bricks they think they will need in these trays

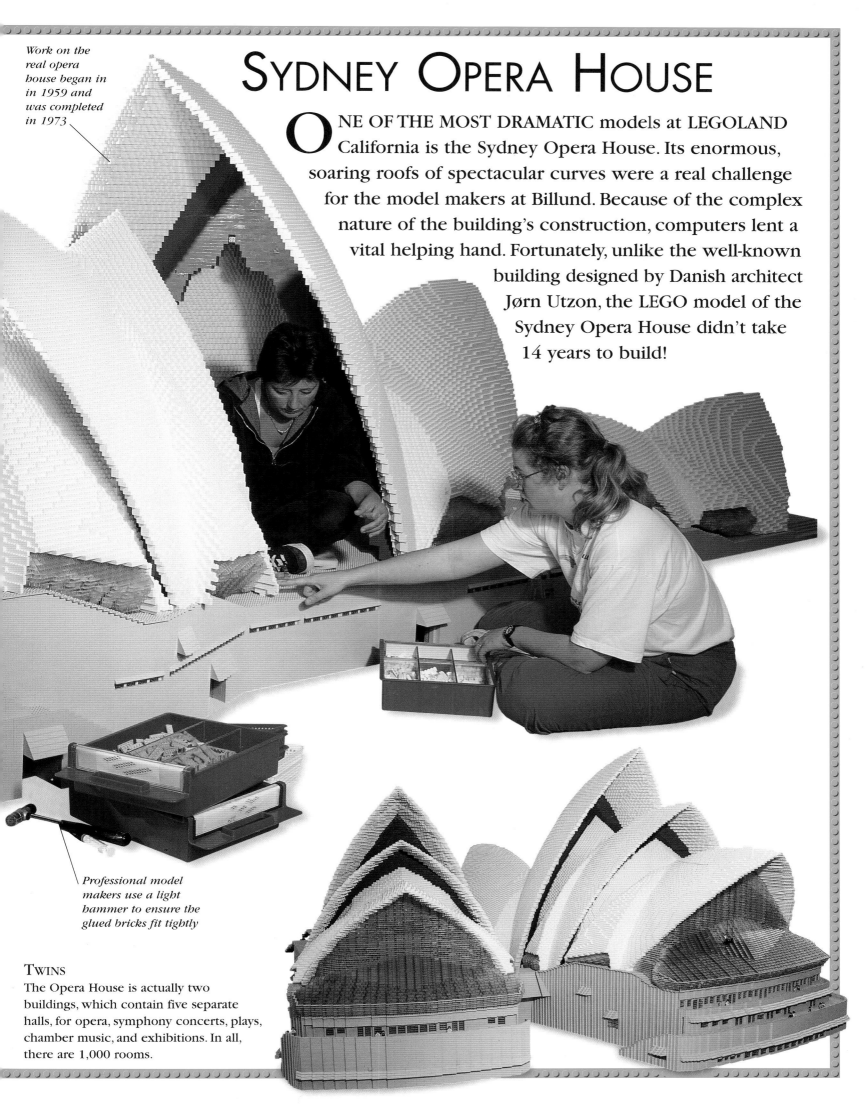

SYDNEY OPERA HOUSE

Work on the real opera house began in in 1959 and was completed in 1973

ONE OF THE MOST DRAMATIC models at LEGOLAND California is the Sydney Opera House. Its enormous, soaring roofs of spectacular curves were a real challenge for the model makers at Billund. Because of the complex nature of the building's construction, computers lent a vital helping hand. Fortunately, unlike the well-known building designed by Danish architect Jørn Utzon, the LEGO model of the Sydney Opera House didn't take 14 years to build!

Professional model makers use a light hammer to ensure the glued bricks fit tightly

TWINS

The Opera House is actually two buildings, which contain five separate halls, for opera, symphony concerts, plays, chamber music, and exhibitions. In all, there are 1,000 rooms.

IMAGINATION UNLIMITED

I N THIS LAST SECTION, we look at the architecture, design, and art that have been inspired by the LEGO System and by LEGO products. The LEGO Group's motto is "Just Imagine …," suggesting that with LEGO elements it is possible to create anything you can dream of. How true is this? Here, we present some of the fruits of LEGO imagination, and we leave you to judge.

WILD WEST CHESS

The figures of this impressive chess set come from the Wild West range. A LEGO chess or draughts set can be made quite easily. You can use figures or animals from any LEGO set as chessmen – or design your own.

This Aztec idol is in the Explorers' Institute at LEGOLAND Windsor

PRIZE PORKER

This personable pig was built by a trainee model maker. You can be sure the modeler went on to a brilliant career!

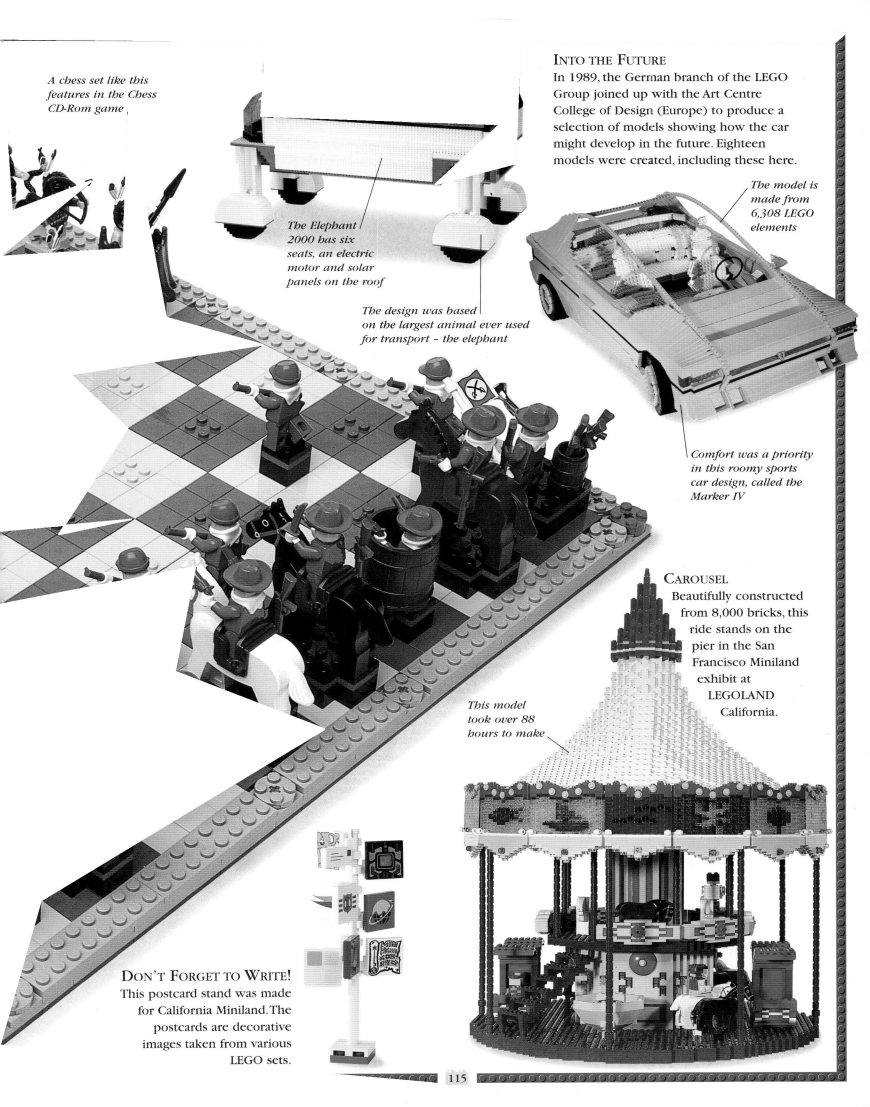

A chess set like this features in the Chess CD-Rom game

INTO THE FUTURE

In 1989, the German branch of the LEGO Group joined up with the Art Centre College of Design (Europe) to produce a selection of models showing how the car might develop in the future. Eighteen models were created, including these here.

The model is made from 6,308 LEGO elements

The Elephant 2000 has six seats, an electric motor and solar panels on the roof

The design was based on the largest animal ever used for transport – the elephant

Comfort was a priority in this roomy sports car design, called the Marker IV

CAROUSEL

Beautifully constructed from 8,000 bricks, this ride stands on the pier in the San Francisco Miniland exhibit at LEGOLAND California.

This model took over 88 hours to make

DON'T FORGET TO WRITE!

This postcard stand was made for California Miniland. The postcards are decorative images taken from various LEGO sets.

THE GATE OF THE PRESENT

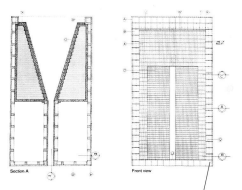

A GATE IS AN EXAMPLE of symbolic architecture, marking a transition from one situation to another. In 1992, the LEGO Group invited architects from 22 countries to design a LEGO model using the gate theme, in this case marking a transition from one time to another. The models were built in Billund to a scale of 54 x 54 x 28 in (135 x 135 x 70 cm) and shown at the Deutsches Architektur Museum in Frankfurt, Germany. The gates reflect not merely the present, but also the past and our expectations for the future.

HOLDING UP HISTORY
This Hungarian design shows the evolution of architecture, from the ancient column to the modern construction that supports it.

Technical drawings show different perspectives of the minimalist gate

The layered gate uses 106,500 LEGO pieces

LAYERS FOR LIFE
This gate designed by Brazilian architects presents itself not as a wall or a door, but as a multitude of layers reflecting the complexity of life.

FUTURE POSSIBILITIES
Designed by Australian architects, this minimalist gate uses 92,660 LEGO bricks. The wide and narrow entrances represent mixed outlooks on the future.

Artist's impression of the moveable layers forming different configurations

Onion-shape dome reflects classic Russian architecture

UNTOUCHABLE TIME
This Greek design represents time as a process. Although the present is the only time that really exists, it is also an untouchable moment. As soon as you realize the present has arrived, it becomes the past.

This gate uses 34,030 LEGO pieces

Artist's impression shows the grandeur of the design

A TIME TO CHOOSE
Elements of the past, present, and future meet in this Russian design. Time is different for each person. With openings both at ground level and on upper levels, you can choose the gate that suits you.

The Russian gate uses 39,840 LEGO pieces

New Visions

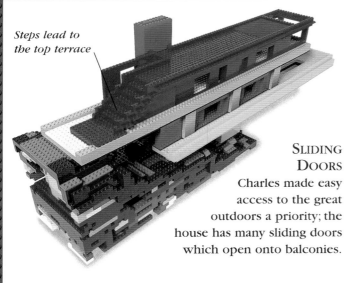

Steps lead to the top terrace

SLIDING DOORS

Charles made easy access to the great outdoors a priority; the house has many sliding doors which open onto balconies.

T HE BEAUTY AND PURITY of nature were architect Charles Tashima's inspiration for his Mountain House model, constructed from LEGO bricks. He would like to locate his dream home high up in the Alps, far, far away from the pollution, congestion, and noise of the big city. "Here, the silence is almost deafening," he comments. "We are in splendid isolation."

ARCHITECT AT WORK
The house has been designed to provide heightened contact with nature.

Charles connects Level 2 on top of Level 1. Level 3 awaits . . .

The primary structure is a cantilever. Like a pier extending into a lake, it is suspended in the air

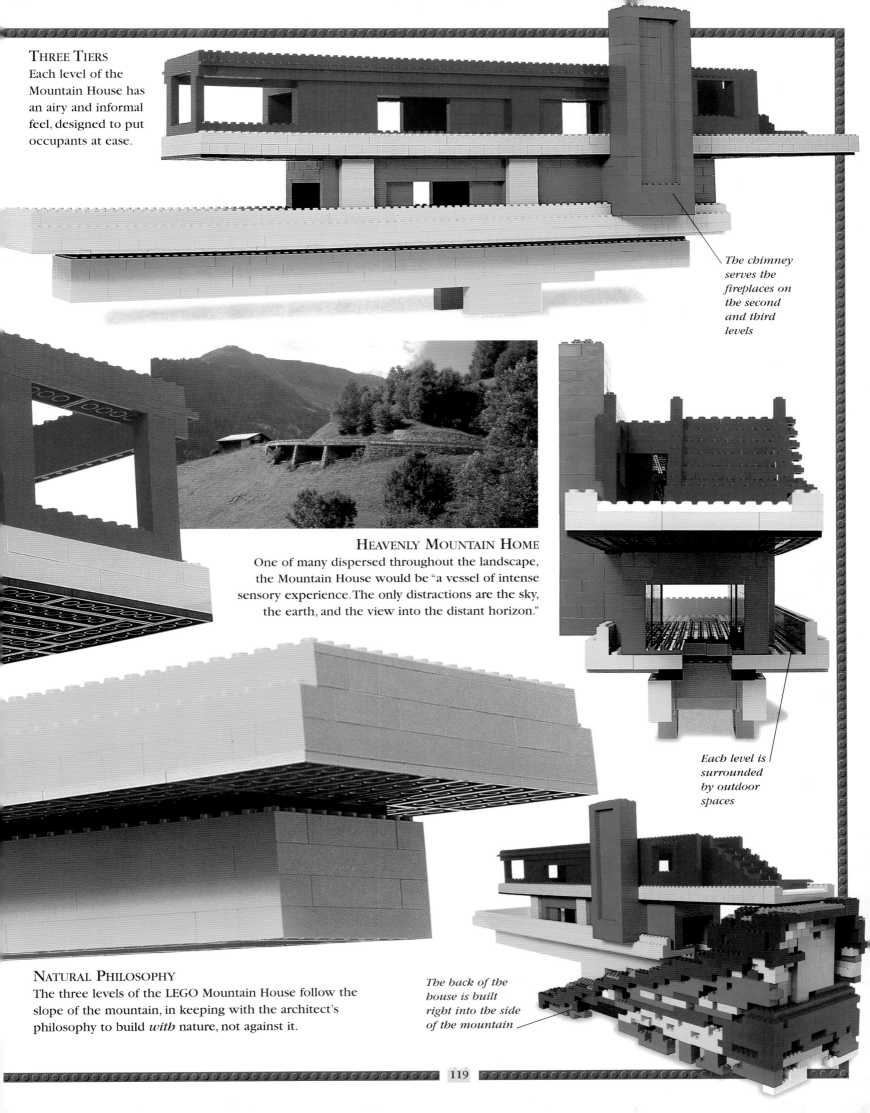

THREE TIERS
Each level of the Mountain House has an airy and informal feel, designed to put occupants at ease.

The chimney serves the fireplaces on the second and third levels

HEAVENLY MOUNTAIN HOME
One of many dispersed throughout the landscape, the Mountain House would be "a vessel of intense sensory experience. The only distractions are the sky, the earth, and the view into the distant horizon."

Each level is surrounded by outdoor spaces

NATURAL PHILOSOPHY
The three levels of the LEGO Mountain House follow the slope of the mountain, in keeping with the architect's philosophy to build *with* nature, not against it.

The back of the house is built right into the side of the mountain

DESIGN DYNAMICS

To DEMONSTRATE the range and flexibilty of LEGO bricks, we asked a designer who specializes in three-dimensional objects to create an object of his choice. Pee Herron has been a fan of LEGO bricks all his life, and he finds that they are an excellent tool to explore all sorts of three-dimensional possibilities.

The visor of the helmet lifts, revealing the wearer's identity

Pee wears his own gear to add to the concept

The face mask has plenty of airholes to allow the wearer to breathe easily

Extra-large pouches hold vital suples

The bags can be adapted in numerous ways to suit the wearer

The ribbed straps allow the bags to be worn on various parts of the body

FORM AND FUNCTION
Pee Herron, 25, studied 3-D design at Leeds Metropolitan University. His approach involves looking at the whole development process, from raw materials through to finished, packaged object. The ergonomic bags illustrated above exemplify his solutions to the problems of transportation and storage on the body.

SCOPE FOR DEVELOPMENT
Pee says, "As a child, LEGO bricks were always one of my favorite toys. As an adult, I have an even greater appreciation of the adaptability, ease of use, and scope for the imagination that are the inherent qualities of LEGO play materials."

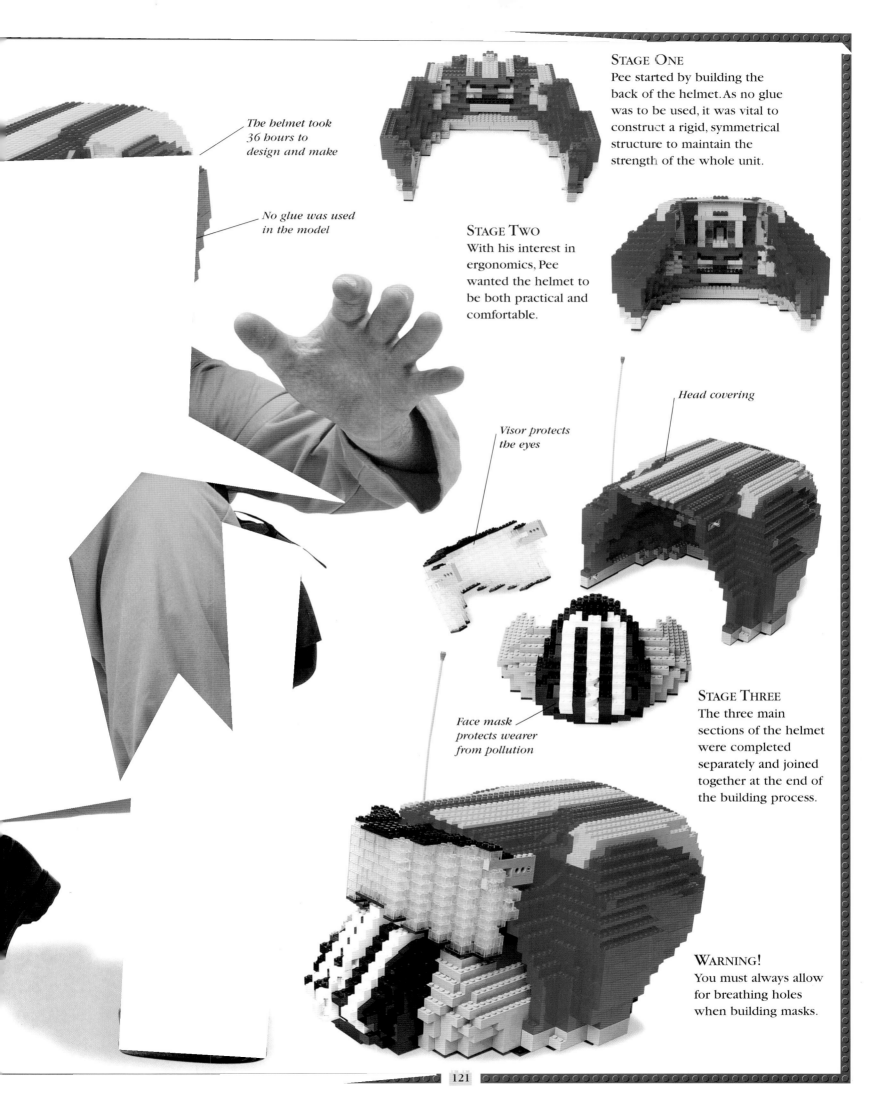

The helmet took
36 hours to
design and make

No glue was used
in the model

STAGE ONE
Pee started by building the
back of the helmet. As no glue
was to be used, it was vital to
construct a rigid, symmetrical
structure to maintain the
strength of the whole unit.

STAGE TWO
With his interest in
ergonomics, Pee
wanted the helmet to
be both practical and
comfortable.

Head covering

Visor protects
the eyes

Face mask
protects wearer
from pollution

STAGE THREE
The three main
sections of the helmet
were completed
separately and joined
together at the end of
the building process.

WARNING!
You must always allow
for breathing holes
when building masks.

FUTURE SCULPTURE

HOW CREATIVE can you be with LEGO bricks? A number of artists from around the world have enjoyed exploring that question. They have yet to find a limit to the answer. To take one example, in 1986 a group of Denmark's most innovative artists worked with LEGO elements to create the Homo Futurus exhibition, imagining and imaging the future in a new way and a new medium – with LEGO bricks. Here are some of the results of their work and vision.

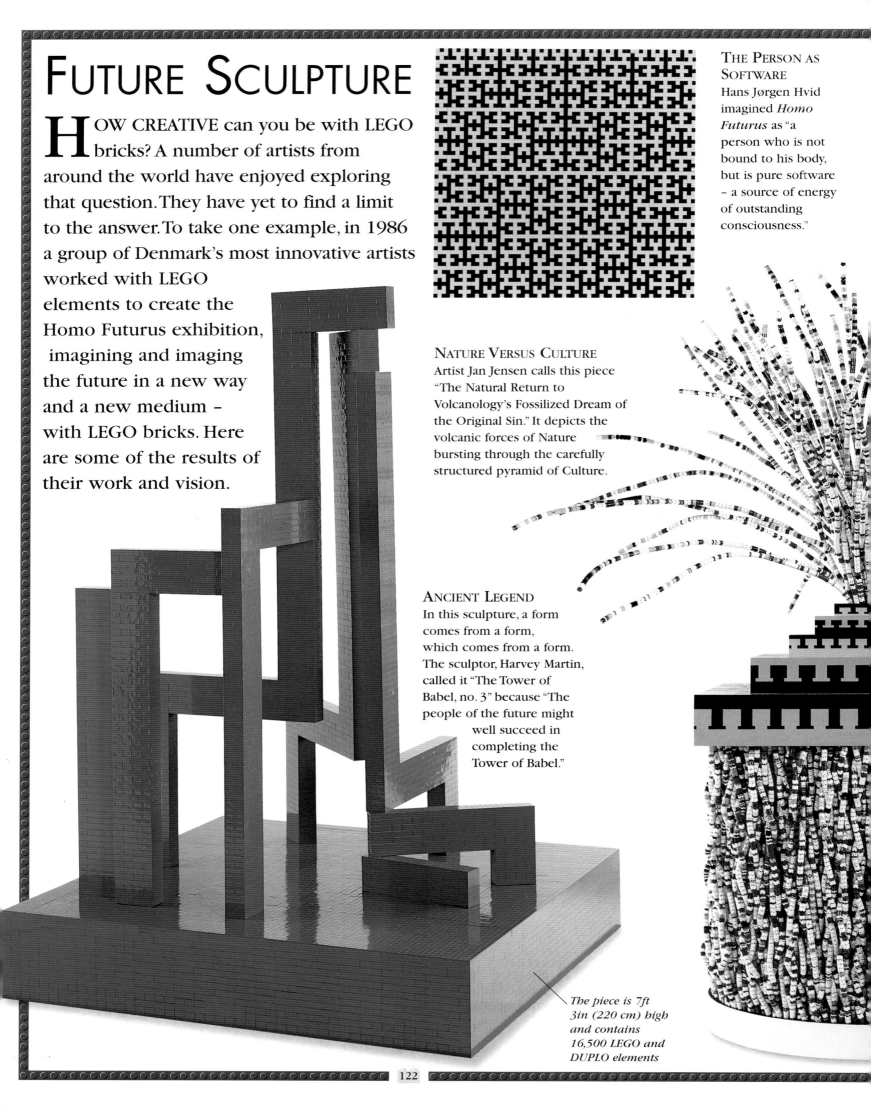

THE PERSON AS SOFTWARE
Hans Jørgen Hvid imagined *Homo Futurus* as "a person who is not bound to his body, but is pure software – a source of energy of outstanding consciousness."

NATURE VERSUS CULTURE
Artist Jan Jensen calls this piece "The Natural Return to Volcanology's Fossilized Dream of the Original Sin." It depicts the volcanic forces of Nature bursting through the carefully structured pyramid of Culture.

ANCIENT LEGEND
In this sculpture, a form comes from a form, which comes from a form. The sculptor, Harvey Martin, called it "The Tower of Babel, no. 3" because "The people of the future might well succeed in completing the Tower of Babel."

The piece is 7ft 3in (220 cm) high and contains 16,500 LEGO and DUPLO elements

"TWO VESSELS"

One vessel is made of blue LEGO bricks and the other of golden straw woven in coiled basketwork – a technique used since ancient times in the Jutland region of Denmark, the home of the LEGO Group. The vessels can be taken to represent the human vessel, the empty vessel awaiting the future to be poured in.

The piece contains about 46,000 LEGO elements

An imaginative mix of elements gives a wonderful textured look to the figure

Culture is depicted as a carefully layered pyramid

The Walker is 6 ft (180 cm) high and contains 120,000 LEGO elements

The figure is 7ft 6in (230 cm) high and contains about 10,000 LEGO elements

"THE WALKER"

The artist Jørn Rønnau made this figure as his idea of the man of the future. Such a person, who seems to be walking but is actually standing still, expresses his ambivalence about the idea of progress: Are we actually progressing, or are we stuck? Can we make progress without doing more harm than good? And can we remain connected to our roots and to the earth as we make progress?

RACIAL FUSION

Per Kramer, its creator, called this sculpture "Joyous Monument to Racial Fusion." In his vision of the future "mankind will go to the stars, frontiers will vanish, the races mix, and the real people of the earth arise."

LEGO Brick Art

ONE OF THE CLAIMS of the LEGO Group is that it has created not just a toy, but something that can be used by children or adults at any level of skill to learn and to express their creativity – in fact, something that cannot be used without being creative, without developing the artist within us. These models pose a challenge to LEGO enthusiasts everywhere.

OLD MASTER
This portrait of the great German Renaissance artist Albrecht Dürer was made for the Nürnburg Toy Fair in 1995. Special squared transparent paper was placed over a poster of the painting to ensure an accurate copy.

LEGO BRICK MASTERPIECE
The Mona Lisa (opposite) was made in 1993 to show how LEGO bricks' basic colors could be used to create remarkably subtle shades.

This portrait of Britain's Queen Elizabeth II was made for the Marché Restaurant at LEGOLAND Windsor

STILL LIFE
This realistic bowl of fruit took more than 40 hours to build using basic LEGO bricks.

A worm is coming out of the apple

INDEX

ACKNOWLEDGMENTS

Picture Credits

The publishers would like to thank the following for their kind permission to reproduce their photographs:

Abbreviations key: t = top, b = bottom, r = right, l = left, c = center

Architectural Association: Peter Jeffree 103bl; **Robert Harding Picture Library:** C Bowman 104tl, 107tr; Ian Robinson 106tl; Philip Craven 105tr; Piers Herron 120bl; DK 46tr, 77br; **Hulton Getty:** 10cl, 10tl, 12cl, 13tr, 15tr; **Images Colour Library:** 97tc, 98tr, 101tr; **Rex Features:** 17tr, Markus Zeffler 21tl; SIPA 20bl; **Science Photo Library:** 11tl, Jerry Mason 23tr; **NASA** 16bl, 18tl; **Novosti** 13cra, 14br; Russell D. Curtis 21br; **Frank Spooner Pictures:** Hoffmann 19tc; **The Stock Market:** 110cr, 112tl; **Tony Stone Images:** Paul Damien 45tr; **Texas Instruments Limited:** 18crb.

**Dorling Kindersley would like to thank
the following LEGO Group employees for their great help
in producing this book:**
Conny Kalcher, Sarah Camburn (LEGO Media International),
Peter Ambeck-Madsen, Anne Mette Dam, Annemarie Kvist,
Eva Lykkegaard (The Information Centre, Billund);
Susanne Ambeck-Madsen (LEGO Licensing, Europe), Vicky Chowdhury
(The LEGO Club UK Marketing), Solveig Ditlevsen, Erik Guldborg,
Birte Nielsen, Otto Juhl Nielsen, Kirsten Martin Stadelhofer
(The LEGO Idea House, Billund), Andrew Peirce, Miriam Evans
(LEGO Licensing UK), Nancy Krieg (LEGOLAND Plannungs GmbH),
Camilla Torpe (LEGOLAND Marketing, Billund), Rachel Townroe
(LEGO Press Office, Windsor), Sue Massey, Peter Roberts, Mark Hamley
(LEGOLAND Attraction Centre, Windsor), Martin Fessel, Jorgen Ranlev
Nielsen (LEGOLAND Attraction Centre, Billund), Preben Dewald,
Jan Harder Blaesild (LEGO Futura, Billund). Pia Norman
(Shows and Events, Billund), Jonna Rae Bartges, Danielle Clare
(LEGOLAND California).

**Dorling Kindersley would also like to thank the
following people:**
Lone Lankjaer Lauritsen from Rosendal, Denmark;
Guy Harvey, Nick Avery, Jane Thomas, Anne Sharples,
Helen Melville, Dominic Zwemmer, John Kelly for design
assistance; Lynn Bresler for the index and proofreading.
Models: Montana Burrett, Oliver Metcalf.